MY LIFE AT CROSSROADS

FOR REG ...
WHO ELSE?

MY LIFE
AT CROSSROADS

by

NOELE GORDON

W. H. ALLEN · LONDON
A division of Howard & Wyndham Ltd.
1975

Printed in Great Britain by
Fletcher & Son Ltd, Norwich for the publishers
W. H. Allen & Co. Ltd, 44 Hill Street, London W1X 8LB
Bound by Richard Clay (The Chaucer Press) Ltd,
Bungay, Suffolk

ISBN 0 491 01602 6

10 Downing Street
Whitehall

I have read this book with great interest and found it amusing and enjoyable. *Crossroads* is a programme which gives a great deal of pleasure to many people. I think that the continuity of the story is a great feature, with new characters being introduced from time to time, and other characters disappearing for a time, to be re-introduced in a natural manner.

I am sure many women see Noele Gordon in the character of Meg Richardson as the type of woman they themselves would like to be—understanding, sensible, able to cope with any situation.

Also, women like to look at Meg's clothes—she is always well-dressed and groomed!

After reading this book, I am now aware of all the work and preparation which goes on behind the scenes.

I have only one complaint about *Crossroads*—I wish that we in London, could have a six months' synopsis to bring us up-to-date with the story, so that we don't have to celebrate Christmas at the motel in the middle of summer!

MARY WILSON

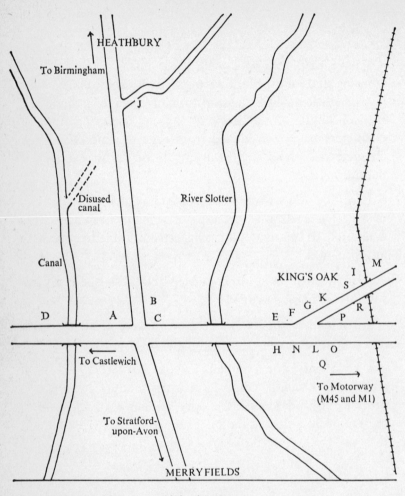

HEATHBURY

To Birmingham

To Castlewich

To Stratford-
upon-Avon

MERRYFIELDS

Disused
canal

Canal

River Slotter

KING'S OAK

To Motorway
(M45 and M1)

A Crossroads Motel
B Cafeteria
C Service station
D Maynard's home
E Rivoli cinema
F Police house
G St Lawrence's
H Diane's home
I Railway station
J Jarvis bungalow

K Amy's cottage
L Archie's cottage
M Fairlawns Hotel
N 'The Running Stag'
O 'The King's Oak'
P 'The Crown'
Q Methodist Chapel
R Post Office
S Antique shop

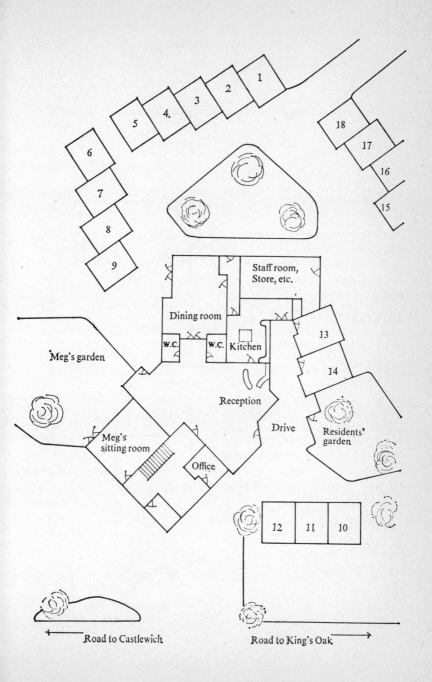

1

2

3

4.

5

6

7

8

9

18

17

16

15

Staff room,
Store, etc.

Dining room

W.C.

W.C.

Kitchen

13

14

Meg's garden

Reception

Drive

Residents'
garden

Meg's
sitting room

Office

12

11

10

Road to Castlewich

Road to King's Oak

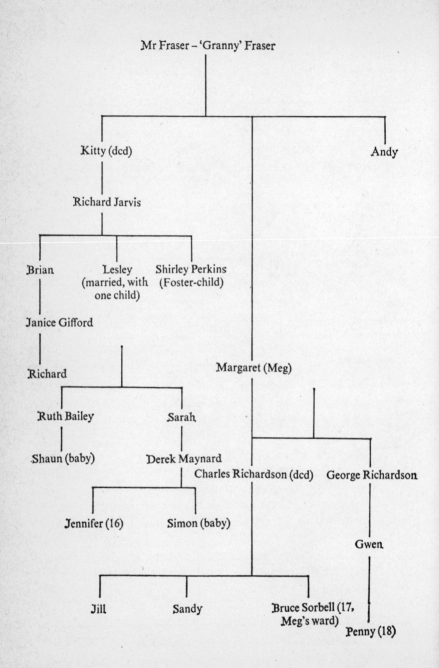

CHAPTER ONE

I am a woman with two lives.

To millions of viewers I am Meg Richardson, the seldom ruffled hostess of *Crossroads*, a Midlands motel. I am so much a part of their life that I even get bookings for my non-existent bedrooms and reservations for my fake dining-room.

People write to me seeking accommodation for overnight stays, holidays and honeymoons. Others even order their wines in advance for their special dinner parties. I just have to write back and gently break the news that *Crossroads*, as a motel, just doesn't exist except in the unreal world of a Birmingham TV studio.

But this is how real *Crossroads* has become for them.

In one sequence David Davenport, as Malcolm Ryder, had to try and poison me. After this episode had been screened, David was in the bar of an hotel at Stratford-upon-Avon when a smartly dressed woman came up to him and hit him over the head with her crocodile handbag.

'How dare you treat Meg like that,' she told him and, from the force of her attack, she obviously meant it.

We have had hotel porters applying for jobs; chamber-maids seeking employment and every year Midlands firms write in for estimates for their annual Christmas staff parties.

One man wanted me to run an hotel in Cornwall that he had just bought.

All this is very understandable, for when I am on the *Crossroads* set in Studio One at ATV's Studio Centre in Birmingham the motel and the life that goes on around it becomes just as real for me as for the viewers.

But away from the studios I become myself again—a professional actress—or at least I try. Though, with this strange double identity, it's astonishing sometimes how the script-writing team, who know nothing of my private life, frequently include dialogue and situations for Meg Richardson which have actually taken place in the life of Noele Gordon.

I will tell you more about these strange coincidences later on. For this is what my book is all about. It will tell the story of *Crossroads*, my life as Meg Richardson, and introduce you to the people who not only work before the cameras but also behind the scenes to make *Crossroads* Britain's most popular TV programme.

I have been Meg Richardson for the past ten years. Apart from the role becoming a way of life for me it has also brought me a unique claim to fame as an actress.

It means that I hold the record for having appeared on TV more often than any other actress in the world. This may not sound very impressive but, believe me, it's extremely exhausting, especially when you realize that *Crossroads* has now passed its 2,000 edition—a world record. I have appeared in almost every episode, apart from when I have been off taking a holiday.

No other performer has been appearing so consistently in a daily TV serial which has run non-stop for so long. The programme is always in the weekly Top Twenty list provided by JICTAR, of Britain's most popular TV programmes. In the *Daily Telegraph* Gallup Poll for 1973 *Crossroads* was named as Britains Most Popular TV Programme and for the past two years readers of the *Sun* newspaper have voted it the best ITV series for the *Sun* Television Awards. *Sun* readers also voted *Crossroads* the second most popular television series—next to *Colditz*. In addition, they voted me as their second favourite TV personality (next to Cilla Black) and the second best actress (next to Googie Withers).

For five years now, readers of the *TV Times* have voted me the most popular woman TV personality on British television and although I don't want to sound egotistical or boastful about all this, the fact remains that it's the loyalty of *Crossroads* fans which have put me there, plus the sincerity and integrity of the programme itself and the people working on it.

If nothing else, *Crossroads* is sincere. We deal with human, contemporary problems. The characters and the situations that surround me are as true to reality as we can make them. This is why people believe in them and why David Davenport was hit over the head with that handbag.

When *Crossroads* began, back in 1964, it made television history as the first daily half-hour TV serial in the world. This, in itself, made it a television phenomenon. It has always been produced on videotape but in the early days it was not technically possible to edit it, as it is now. There could be no 'stop and start' production schedule on the studio floor as with a filmed serial. If I muffed my lines or any of the cast found themselves in difficulties with their words or positioning, then the whole programme had to be stopped and started again. With our new videotape editing equipment, scenes which go wrong can now be cut out and taped again.

Crossroads has become a four-day-a-week serial, screened throughout the ITV network, and also shown in Australia, and Hong Kong.

So now let me tell you how it all started ...

Crossroads really began back in 1959 or, at least, the idea for a daily serial started then. In those days I used to be hostess on ITV's first Midlands chat show—*Lunch Box*. We had a resident team and I had celebrities to interview. The show was produced in ATV's old Aston Road studios on the outskirts of Birmingham and it had a big following. As the show grew more popular we used to take it out on location. At our first outside broadcast Sir Lew Grade watched the programme in his London office beamed to him directly by landline from our Midlands studios.

All our shows were live, nothing was recorded, so the

11

idea of taking a live TV programme on tour immediately appealed to Sir Lew's show-biz know-how.

But what really impressed him were the 27,000 fans who turned up at Nottingham Forest football ground to see the programme. We had expected about 3,000.

When I walked out on the soccer pitch they gave me the kind of cheer you usually only hear at Wembley.

We used to have our own 'Birthday Time' and 'Happy Anniversary' signature tunes on the show and the crowd stood up and sang them to us. It really was a fantastic moment. Then they stormed over the barricades and ran across the grass for my autograph. I was mobbed. Sir Lew, and other ATV executives, watching the relay over close circuit to London were astonished. Just as I was.

None of us quite realized what an impact *Lunch Box* was having on Midlanders and, as the hostess on the show, I had obviously become the Midland's first TV star—something that just had not happened in BBC days before the start of commercial television.

It was this quite unexpected reception that I had from those warm-hearted folk that made *Crossroads* possible later on and I will always be grateful to them.

Sir Lew Grade was soon on the phone to Reg Watson, who was then producing *Lunch Box*.

'Can you do one of those outside broadcasts a week?' he asked our Brisbane-born producer.

'Not really,' Reg told him. 'We haven't the staff or the facilities, but we'll do as many as we can. What I'd really like to do is a daily serial.'

'You mean like those American soap operas?' said Sir Lew.

'No,' replied Reg. 'I don't mean an American soap opera. They only go out twice a week. I mean a real daily serial. It must be a daily.'

Nothing more was said. But Sir Lew is a man who never forgets a good idea.

Five years later (!), on an August Bank Holiday, I had a phone call at my house at Ross-on-Wye from Philip Dorte who was then ATV's Midlands Controller. I was just leaving to go to Birmingham to appear on *Lunch Box*.

'Nolly,' he said, 'I want to see you. Can you drop in on your way back from the studios?'

That evening I stopped off at Philip's home and the first thing he did was to give me a drink.

'I've got a shock for you,' he said. 'They're taking off *Lunch Box*.'

I felt myself go a little white. There was a sinking feeling in my tummy. *Lunch Box* had been my life for eight years. It was a terrible blow to suddenly hear it was all going to end. I was so stunned I scarcely heard Philip's next words:

'But don't worry,' he said, 'it's going to be replaced with a new half-hour daily serial—and you're going to be the woman in it.'

I sat down. I couldn't believe what I had heard. At that time the only serial on British commercial television was *Coronation Street*—but only two programmes a week. The idea of producing a TV drama serial every day had never been attempted.

'Who's going to produce it?' I asked.

'Reg Watson,' Philip told me.

'Well,' I said, 'it's something he's always wanted.'

This, then, is how *Crossroads* was born.

The script team of Hazel Adair and Peter Ling were brought in and they made me the central character—the owner of a Midlands motel. They built all the other characters around me and I became Meg Richardson. In fact, I've been Meg Richardson ever since.

Originally, Peter Ling and Hazel Adair had submitted an outline for a serial which they had called *The Midland Road*. But the situation was the same—a somewhat impoverished widow faced with the problem of bringing up two children and running a motel, which she had made out of the manor house left her by her husband.

The whole idea of the serial was to provide the Midlands viewers with a story set in the Midlands itself. There was also the chance of getting the serial taken up by other ITV

13

companies, so this meant a wonderful opportunity to project the Midlands image to the rest of Britain.

Coronation Street was covering Lancashire and the North, and I suppose you could say that the twice-weekly hospital series *Emergency–Ward 10* had done the same for the South which, incidentally, Sir Lew Grade dropped and has regretted ever since.

But *Coronation Street* centred on smoking chimneys, cloth caps and terraced houses. There was no real cross-section of everyday life and certainly no one had yet tried to cater for Midlanders.

The first problem was to decide just who the Midlanders really were, for our viewing area covered Swindon, Stoke, and the Black Country. We also extended south to Oxford and covered the borders of Anglia, as well as part of Yorkshire and Lancashire. So although *Crossroads* was to be for Midlanders it couldn't just appeal to Birmingham viewers alone. It had to have a much broader basis.

Having decided to take the idea put up for the serial by Hazel Adair and Peter Ling, we then set about trying to get the right title.

The Midland Road somehow didn't seem to have much of an impact so ATV ran a competition in a Midlands newspaper in the hope of someone coming up with a bright idea. As it happened, none of the entries suited us either—so the prize we had offered went to charity.

Finally, from a number of suggestions put forward by Reg Watson himself, it was decided to take the title of *Crossroads*.

'It's the one everyone likes the most,' said Reg, 'so let's settle for that.'

From then on the whole concept of *Crossroads* was kept very quiet and we were all sworn to secrecy. We in ITV are, after all, in competition with the BBC in the battle for viewers and so this became ATV's top secret project.

But as auditions got under way to choose the rest of the cast, news of what we had in mind filtered through to the BBC.

One of our young actresses met a BBC official at a party and he said to her, 'I hear ATV are to produce a daily TV serial. It's absolute rubbish. They'll never do it.'

'You're wrong,' she told him quietly. 'We've already got the first two weeks in the can.' And in November 1964 our first episode went on the air.

But they were hectic days. I had had plenty of television experience as a personality—hostess of my own daily TV show—but none as a TV actress.

Lunch Box had then been running for eight years and as the hostess, I had faced the camera for every programme, apart from holidays. But the big difference between *Lunch Box* and *Crossroads* was that, for the first time on television, I had to give up being myself.

Let me tell you what I mean. Michael Parkinson, Hughie Green, Eamonn Andrews, Russell Harty, and other personalities always appear as *themselves*. And if a performer has a pleasant, natural manner then it's not too difficult to become a TV personality as well.

Of course, you have to acquire the tricks of the trade—how to interview; how to face the camera; how to cover up when things go wrong, and so on. But once you have mastered this technique then the actual TV performance isn't such an ordeal.

Back in the early fifties I had been to the United States for a year to study television and work in a big New York studio. As far as I know, I was the only English actress to do this when commercial television was first approved by Parliament.

I realized that the old theatrical life I had known—of musical plays, variety, and music halls—would gradually be superseded by the new medium of television. This decided me to go to New York and learn what I could about TV production and the presentation of programmes.

My hunch paid off. For when I returned to England with this background, I was offered a job on the staff of ATV and I have worked for them ever since.

First of all I began as a trainee director and adviser on

15

women's programmes, then I went to Birmingham to help launch our five-days-a-week operation which ATV then had.

We opened up in February 1956 and my first office was a dressing-room at the Theatre Royal, the same theatre where I had made my final stage appearance two years previously before deciding to quit and take a chance with a new career in commercial television.

But I didn't stay an executive for long. In our first week of transmission I was on the air with a chat show *Tea with Noele Gordon* in which I interviewed visiting theatrical personalities.

This made me something of a TV personality myself. The viewers seemed to like me and the ratings were good, so I stayed on the screen as a performer.

From *Tea with Noele Gordon* I moved in as hostess of *Lunch Box*, ITV's first lunch-time variety and chat show.

This is really what distinguishes me from the rest of the *Crossroads* cast—I am the only one to be on the staff of ATV as opposed to actors and actresses who are only engaged for individual programmes or series.

Again, as far as I know, I am also the only actress to be on the staff of any TV organization—ITV or BBC.

It was with this kind of background that I approached the role of Meg Richardson. It was a great worry to me and I spent many sleepless nights over it. For till now, I had always been myself on the screen; now I had to be Meg Richardson, someone quite different.

There was the awful fear—could I learn lines again? For eight years I had worked in television as myself—everything in *Lunch Box* was *ad lib*. We never had cue sheets. We never had scripts. The shows were live, not recorded. So if things went wrong, it was up to me to cover up.

As Meg Richardson I not only had to become a character—a widow with a teenage son and daughter—but I also had to learn the lines she had to say—and put the right emphasis on them. I would also have to register the many emotions that Meg Richardson would be bound to have in

16

her involvements with her staff and guests, as well as her private life.

For there is another great difference between hosting a show like Mike Parkinson's interview programme and playing a dramatic part in a TV play.

As a personality you play *into* the camera. You treat the camera as a viewer; you take it into your confidence; you exchange intimacies with it. In short, you talk to the camera as though it is a real person.

It is the ability to do this, to make friends with the camera and use it to convey your own genuineness and sincerity, that makes or breaks you as a TV personality. For it is the camera which represents the viewer and if the viewer doubts your sincerity, you can pack up and go home. You're finished.

But *acting* for TV is something very different. As Meg Richardson I had to do exactly the opposite. I had to *forget* the camera. To ignore its existence.

Like any other TV actress, I had to put myself into the character I was playing and think of nothing else. It then becomes the director's responsibility to catch my moods; my expressions; my unspoken thoughts with his own subtle use of the camera. My job is to play the part—his job is to cover everything I do.

So my great fear remained—could I become someone else? In this case, Meg Richardson. Could I become this other woman so convincingly that viewers would accept me as such?

If I failed, the whole of *Crossroads* would fail too. For unless viewers could forget Noele Gordon and accept me as Meg Richardson, the owner of a Midlands motel, then they wouldn't believe in *Crossroads*.

This is what scared me stiff. But at the same time, I kept telling myself that I was after all, an actress. I'd been trained at RADA. I knew my job. I'd starred in the West End. It was too late now to turn back.

Before any TV scripts are actually written for a series the producer and the writers have to agree on what we call

17

story lines. These are the outlines for the plots around which the dialogue has to be written.

When *Crossroads* first began, Reg Watson decided there would be only two story lines. One of these involved my running of the motel and the other centred on the shop run by my sister. And this is how it was—with only ten in the cast—for the first three months.

Nowadays, many TV series and serials make the mistake of starting off with too many such situations. Audiences get muddled. They can't remember who is who or what is what. I'm sure the reason why many of our imitators have failed is because, from the start, they had too many situations or involvements happening at once.

In *Crossroads* we now have up to six different story lines going at once. But our audiences have become accustomed to this—they can follow what is happening as different developments take place. If we had begun with six story lines when we first went on the air there would have been a mass switch off.

I took the first story line with me on one of my two annual visits to Forest Mere, the health clinic at Liphook in Hampshire. For now I'm going to let you into a secret. I have been going there regularly for years because, like most small women, weight has always been a problem to me.

TV always puts on pounds. You can reckon that most people look at least half a stone to a stone heavier on the screen than they are in real life. Don't ask me why—it's just one of the mysteries of the camera. It fattens you up. It's most unfair really, but it is so. This is why many performers have to slip away just as I do, and slim themselves down.

It also explains why viewers often write to me just before I leave the programme for my bi-annual slimming and tell me how plump I am looking. I always write back and tell them I'm not as plump as all that! And then, of course, they worry again on my return:

'Dear Meg,' they write, 'you are losing weight. Are you sure you're getting enough to eat?'

I assure them that I am—and let it go at that.

But now you all know what really happens to me when I'm missing for that odd week, twice a year. The script-writers just write Meg Richardson out of the series; viewers think I'm on holiday or visiting friends.

I don't only go to Forest Mere to lose weight, even though I can shed as much as a stone sometimes. It is also to clear the system and recharge the batteries.

We work at a tremendous pace on the serial, and I'm quite sure it's the fasting, massage, and the rest of the health treatment that I get every six months which keeps me going.

Mind you, I'm in good company. Many other stars go there as well—Eamonn Andrews, Ronnie Corbett, Ava Gardner, Sean Connery, Hayley Mills, and so on.

We all need to keep slim, look fit, and stay healthy, and this is how we do it.

On my last visit to Forest Mere I weighed eight stone, ten and a half pounds. After a week's stay I had lost eight pounds. So you see, it *does* work. At least it does in my case. But I wouldn't advise dieting or fasting except under proper medical supervision. It works with me, but only because I put myself in the hands of experts.

And it was while I was in their hands that I took out those first foolscap pages marked 'Confidential—Copyright ATV'.

I saw from the start that Reg Watson had the right approach. The settings were plain and uncomplicated for, again, a TV screen isn't like the stage or the cinema. It is so much smaller and people cannot move around in the same way; this is why all the big epic feature films with their casts of thousands are quite wasted when seen within the tiny confines of television. With *Crossroads* we have realized this from the start. The sets are simple—deliberately so, and as members of the cast, our movements are cut to a minimum.

Fresh from Forest Mere, I returned to Birmingham and for the next three months we were all plunged into the most hectic and exhausting work I have ever known.

19

The time-table which Reg had devised was ingenious and demanding. At the end of each day I was so tired I could hardly find the energy to talk and I'm sure it was the same for the rest of the cast.

As a young girl I had done my stint of repertory—where you rehearse one play a week while performing another at night—but with *Crossroads* it was much tougher. Not only did we have to learn the equivalent of a full-length play every week but we also had to rehearse and tape five programmes.

We used to get every Sunday free, but that's all. And by free I just mean away from the studio. During this 'freedom' most of us were still learning our lines. One episode was recorded on Tuesday afternoon; two more on Wednesday and two more on Thursday. We rehearsed on Friday, Saturday, and Monday.

This kind of life was tougher than anyone else had ever experienced in British television. None of us had any social life. We just worked and slept; we lived in a twilight world of TV studios and rehearsal rooms. We had no other interests in life—we were TV zombies.

I am not complaining, but believe me, looking back, those days were the toughest I have ever had in the whole of my professional career. But on this conveyor belt principle, never used before in British television, *Crossroads* became a hit.

At the start, apart from the Midlands, which is ATV's own area, only two other ITV areas took the programme—Ulster and Border. Then gradually, as audiences built up in these three areas, other ITV companies joined in the networking. One of the last to hold out was Granada in Lancashire where, understandably, they regarded us as something of a rival to their own twice-weekly serial *Coronation Street*. But in 1972 Granada joined in and now our serial is seen throughout Britain.

Gradually, as the series has progressed, so the pace has slackened. More characters have been brought in and more story lines developed. Then it was cut down from five episodes a week to four. This has made things much easier all round. Characters get 'rested' and written out of the scripts for a while and newcomers are brought in. Even so, each programme covers thirty-five pages of foolscap and, usually, ten separate scenes. Each episode generally has me in four scenes, so all this has to be learned—that's sixteen scenes a week.

Still it's a routine and I'm used to it so that now, like so many viewers, life without *Crossroads* just wouldn't be the same.

CHAPTER TWO

They have a nickname for me on the *Crossroads* set, they call me 'The Godmother' and I sign myself 'The Godmother' on my Christmas cards.

For this is really what I am. Roger Tonge, who plays my son, and Jane Rossington, who appears as my daughter, are the only ones remaining from the original cast who still appear regularly.

But there are three others who were also with us in Episode One and they return from time to time. These are David Fennell, who appears as Brian Jarvis, Meg's nephew; Peggy Aitchison, who plays Mrs Blundel, wife of a local farmer who does occasional work as a home help in the motel, and Alan Haywood who has had several roles. Originally, he was Frank Gillow, boss of a local construction gang.

But Roger and Jane are the closest to me. They have grown up with the show from teenagers to adults, just like any family in real life.

Neither of them had any experience of television when we started, and just as I did my best to help them in our early days together, so I now do what I can to give practical help and encouragement to the many newcomers when they first arrive before the cameras.

I know our critics sometimes make fun of that dead, glazed look that comes into the eyes of some of our cast. Well, they're right. We all get the glazed look sometimes— glazed with fear.

There is nothing more terrifying for an actor to be in front of a camera, knowing the whole scene is depending on your next words and then to forget your lines.

Every actor is petrified of drying up for it usually results in the Dead Look in the eyes and for any actor to have dead, expressionless eyes is just about the worst thing that can happen to him. Tell any actor his eyes were dead while playing any role and he'll hate you for life.

When this kind of catastrophe hits you in a TV studio you have the choice of either stopping completely (which means the whole scene has to be shot again) or you can say a little prayer that someone else who is in that particular scene with you will realize your predicament, come to your rescue, and cover up for you.

This is normal theatrical custom and it happens both on the stage and in films, but on TV, when so much is shot in close-up, the audience is much more aware of facial reactions.

Our directors expect us to be word perfect and we all do our best but sometimes we fail, so forgive us our glazed look occasionally, now that you know what it's all about.

We have always tried to give a start to young unknown performers in addition to guest appearances by top TV names such as Larry Grayson, Ken Dodd, Bob Monkhouse, Tony Britton, Stan Stenett, and Shaw Taylor. After all, you can't run a motel, even an imaginary one, with the same staff for ever and ever and the guests themselves must come and go as well.

More than 10,000 actors and actresses have worked with me on the series and, for many of them, it was not only their first job straight out of drama school, but also their first TV appearance.

As the most experienced TV actress around the *Crossroads* rehearsal room, the youngsters naturally come to me with their problems and this is how I acquired 'The Godmother' label. For there are not only dramas in our scripts; we get plenty of backstage problems too, and it's 'The Godmother' who is usually consulted.

We used to have a role of a young schoolgirl which was played by a teenage actress. She had quite a following among viewers but one day she came to me in tears and told me she was expecting a baby—so we had to write her out of the story and she left.

The part was then reshaped and given to another young teenage actress and she too appeared on the screen as a schoolgirl. Within a few weeks the new arrival took me into a corner and—again in tears—told me that she too would have to leave—for the same reason as her predecessor!

Reg and I then decided that the role must have some kind of motherhood hoodoo on it and it was quietly dropped.

The human problems and dramas of *Crossroads* are not confined to Meg's motel.

On the other hand, there are many happy moments and success stories too.

We have been fortunate to help launch several stars. They had their first break with *Crossroads* and worked with us when they were quite unknown.

One big success has been achieved by Jon Finch, now a top box-office attraction in international films. Jon came to us as a very raw, inexperienced player in our early days to make his début in six programmes starting with Episode 947. He played the role of Gareth Leyton, a somewhat weird and slightly off-beat character.

He had a tremendous assurance and flair before the cameras and it came as no surprise to us when he hit the headlines as a world star.

Roman Polanski picked him for his film version of *Macbeth*, Alfred Hitchcock chose him to star in *Frenzy*, and he had a leading role in Robert Bolt's *Lady Caroline Lamb* as well as the slightly effeminate hero of *The Final Programme* for which he had to wear black nail polish and a flared Edwardian style coat.

However, I'm pleased that Jon Finch is now returning to the Midlands. As Robin Hood he'll be leading his merry men around Nottingham's Sherwood Forest for his next film.

Malcolm McDowell—son of a Leeds publican and now

also in the superstar class—made his first TV appearance in *Crossroads* when he was twenty years old and quite unknown. He began a little earlier than Jon Finch—in Episode 643.

He had the role of Crispin Ryder, a public relations consultant. Just a small part, but he was very effective.

Today, at twenty-nine, Malcolm is one of the most sought after young actors in the world—following his electrifying performance in Stanley Kubrick's *A Clockwork Orange* when he played the part of Alex, the violent Teddy Boy hero, who beat up Adrienne Corri.

He came to us after throwing in his job as a coffee salesman and working in a repertory company at the Pavilion, Shanklin. He had also carried a spear with the Royal Shakespeare Company.

After *Crossroads* he was in several TV series—*Dixon of Dock Green, Z Cars*, and *Emergency–Ward 10*.

While he was at the Royal Court he was auditioned by Lindsay Anderson who gave him the starring role of a schoolboy revolutionary in the film *If*. His latest film, *Oh, Lucky Man* revived that association.

Roy Holder—who comes from Aston—worked on *Crossroads* as a non-speaking boy extra. This was his first TV work and he had the part of a newsboy—selling evening papers.

From *Crossroads*, as a fifteen-year-old, he landed a plum role in the Elizabeth Taylor–Richard Burton film *Taming of the Shrew*, playing the part of the boy urchin, Biondello. The production was filmed in Italy and distributed here by Columbia–Warner.

Another young teenager who came to us and later found fame is Penny Spencer, the sexy Sharon from *Please Sir* and *The Fenn Street Gang*.

Penny had been in a *Dixon of Dock Green* episode for the BBC as a witness in a court scene but in *Crossroads* she had her first real chance as an actress.

She played the part of Muriel, Meg's secretary. In the script, Muriel was a rather dull, unattractive girl, but when

Penny turned up we saw at once it would be very hard for viewers to accept her as such.

So we changed things and made her a dizzy blonde. And Penny played it for laughs. She did everything wrong. She couldn't type, she couldn't do shorthand, but she did manage to fall in love with Peppi, one of the chefs.

This was Penny's first experience of working in a TV serial. She had tried for a place at RADA without success but had been well trained at a drama school in Surrey. She was with us for two weeks and it was soon after she was seen on the screen as my secretary, that she was snapped up by London Weekend Television to become one of the stars of *Please Sir*.

Peppi, incidentally, was played by Stephen Rea who has also made quite a niche for himself.

Viewers saw him in ATV's Saturday night Thriller series playing opposite Gayle Hunnicutt as a man and wife detective team in *K is for Killing*. This series will also be screened in the USA.

He had the leading role of Donal Daren in the BBC2 production of *Shadow of a Gunman*. At the same time as he was on TV in *Thriller* he was also appearing in the Sam Shepard play *Geography of a Horse Dreamer* at the Royal Court.

Wendy Padbury—well known for her appearances as Zoe in the BBC's *Dr Who* and three series of *The Freewheelers* for Southern Television—also had her TV start with us.

Wendy is now married and has a three-months-old daughter. Her husband is actor Melvin Hayes who was in the BBC's comedy army series *It Ain't Half Hot, Mum* with Michael Bates.

She came to *Crossroads* after touring in the Anthony Newley musical *War of the Greasepaint, Smell of the Crowd*.

Trained by Aida Foster, Wendy was then seventeen and had to appear with me as Stevie Harris, a girl of fourteen who had come from a broken home. Meg had to look after her and become her foster mother.

Wendy who was born at Stratford-upon-Avon, stayed with her parents who were still living there and used to travel over to our Birmingham studios.

She really knew nothing about television, although she was an accomplished singer and had, in fact, been placed second in an ITV talent show *Search for a Star*, produced by Elkan Allen, now the TV critic of the *Sunday Times*. In those days Elkan was variety chief for Rediffusion Ltd, which had the ITV week-day contract for the London area.

Wendy was with *Crossroads* for seven months and I know she learned a great deal. She gave us a good laugh one day when, in one scene with Carlo, the chef, he had to give her a boiled egg to eat. Wendy didn't bother to eat the egg at rehearsals but when it came to the actual transmission she put her spoon in her egg, dipped it in the salt, and took the first mouthful.

None of us knew what had happened—Wendy didn't bat an eyelid. It wasn't until later that we learned her boiled egg was actually stinking—quite bad!

Wendy, however, was brave enough to carry on. While the cameras were turning she carried on with her dialogue as though she was enjoying every mouthful and, somehow, managed to eat her bad egg at the same time. That's dedication for you!

Although now married, with a baby of her own, she is still specializing in children's parts. I saw her the other day as a fourteen-year-old girl in one of Granada's *Crown Court* episodes. I had always thought it was Peter Pan who was never supposed to grow up—in real life, it's Wendy as well.

Anne Stallybrass successfully auditioned for us but we were not able to fit her into the programme at that time and she went on to star in *The Onedin Line* for the BBC, and *The Strauss Family* musical for ATV.

Daniel Thorndike, nephew of Dame Sybil Thorndike, played the part of an odd-job man. Daniel, who spent nine years with the London Old Vic Company is the son of Russell Thorndike, creator of the Dr Syn historical thrillers.

Ken Dodd made his TV début on *Crossroads* as a straight actor. He was really there in the guise of an hotel guest. We had lunched together first and, unfortunately, turned up half an hour late for the recording so we could only have twenty minutes rehearsal.

He was great fun to work with and the idea was that I should go along to his chalet on the day he was leaving the motel and get him to deliver some parcels for me.

At the start, Doddy played it straight but then he went after the laughs. At one point the technicians were laughing so much they could hardly continue. Doddy claimed to have written to Downing Street demanding fair play for all his Noddy constituents at Knotty Ash. He was particularly keen on securing ladders for them for parking meters.

I just let him take over. We had worked together often in the past in my *Lunch Box* days so that I knew what to expect. In fact, he made his first-ever TV appearance with me back in the fifties.

He is a great natural clown and he had even brought along a special Yorick's clown for a cod Hamlet speech. It had square eye sockets.

'That's from watching too much TV,' he explained.

But despite the stars we've found, and the established performers who have worked with us, as a programme it is fair to say that no show has been more maligned, thrashed, or just plain criticized than *Crossroads*.

Ted Rogers, compère of *Sunday Night at the London Palladium*, has been making jokes about us on stage and TV for years. But not always successfully.

At one of his appearances on a variety bill at the London Palladium with Tom Jones, he came on with his usual mickey-taking remarks about the programme. I know he meant it in good fun. But he got a swift response from some of our fans in the audience.

'Nothing wrong with *Crossroads*,' one woman in the stalls shouted back at him.

Ted rose to the occasion.

'Oh,' he said to her from the stage, 'you like it then?'

'Yes, we do,' some of our fans shouted back in chorus. 'Leave *Crossroads* alone.'

And Ted went on to tell jokes about something else.

Well, I would be the first to say that all is not perfect with our serial. Of course some of the cast make mistakes. Of course many professional critics regard *Crossroads* as banal. But then the serial was never designed to please professional journalists. It *was* designed to appeal to millions of men and women who want to watch a homely, but authentic story of everyday happenings in a Midlands motel.

Our viewing figures—a regular 14,000,000 for each programme—prove that we have the right approach and although over the years there have been many imitators, none of them has had the same impact and none has lasted.

Back in 1966, Kenneth Eastaugh once wrote in the *Daily Mirror*: 'Everybody and everything moves in agonizing slow motion, dragging every petty incident to the point where it snaps and vanishes. The dialogue is woolly, the acting stilted, the directing stale, the result absurd.'

Now Mr Eastaugh is perfectly entitled to say such things just as I'm entitled to point out that he is now no longer with the *Daily Mirror*. He left for the *Sun*. He is now no longer with the *Sun*.

But *Crossroads* is in its tenth year.

Even so, the critics still knock us. We came in for some harsh words from Richard Afton in the London *Evening News*. His article was also reprinted in the *Birmingham Evening Mail*.

Mr Afton is one of the pioneers of British television and responsible for a number of top productions during his days as a BBC variety producer.

He produced shows like *TV Music Hall*, *Top Hat Rendezvous*, *Quite Contrary*, and *Come Dancing*—perhaps not the epitome of sophisticated entertainment. But they did have a mass appeal and large numbers of viewers, millions of them, found these shows both entertaining and enjoyable.

29

However his contract was not renewed and unlike many of his BBC colleagues, he has never been employed by any of the ITV companies. In fact for some years now, Mr Afton has had to use his skill as a producer and director in other fields. He no longer works in television.

This being so, I was somewhat surprised to pick up our local evening paper and find that he had made an astonishing and quite vitriolic attack on some of us who are still working in the medium which no longer employs him.

Here's what he had to say about us:

The intellectual level of TV would be raised if that deep depression over the centre of England called 'Crossroads' was to be set adrift in the highways and byways of the Midlands with guide, map or compass.

It might, with luck, get lost forever.

This dreary soap opera, churning out its miseries and woes four nights a week, must be responsible for as much gloom in the households who watch the show as a Harold Wilson speech.

More so, because sometimes Mr Wilson is very funny, although he doesn't intend to be.

The stories are trite and the situations contrived.

Gimmick

Whenever they can they resort to the juvenile gimmick of terminating an episode with a 'cliffhanger' similar to the Saturday afternoon serials at the pictures fifty years ago.

It would be difficult to find a worse acted show on TV than this one.

It is on a par with Junior Showtime and you cannot get much worse than that.

Weary Willie Harvey—with his flat 'at which, I am sure, is glued on as he rarely removes it—grumbles on and on and gives the impression that his idea of a hilarious time is going to funerals.

Tired Tim Sandy, with the weight of the world on his shoulders, drones on in his monotonous whining way and never smiles.

He looks as if he is the most unhappy young man in the country.

Maybe the wheelchair is getting him down.

As for scandal-mongering Amy, she should join the other two old ladies locked in the lavatory.

It would stop her tongue wagging for a time and she might even learn her lines.

Lording it over all is Saint Meg. I am sure she will be canonized some day ... she is just too good and saintly to be true.

In these troubled times, do viewers really want to be subjected, month after month, to the sordid misfortunes of fictitious people?

Are we so sadistic?

I realize that they will quote the 'ratings', but these are no real criterion.

System

A comparatively small number of machines attached to sets scattered around the country, plus a modicum of interviews, which is the system employed, is no consensus of mass public opinion in Britain.

In any event, the machines themselves are no real guide. They only record at what time the set was switched on and to what channel.

They cannot register if anyone was watching or what they thought of the show if they were.

Afton's attack is quite the worst we've ever had. We're used to the occasional blasts from the critics but this was something rather different. From a former colleague this was a calculated diatribe that, in its content, was both vicious and destructive.

His onslaught caused a furore. The *Birmingham Mail* was flooded with letters. They printed a selection for two days running and the editor acknowledged that the letters were firmly 3–1 in our favour.

This cheered us all up no end.

And we took some added consolation in the knowledge that *Crossroads* continues—whereas Mr Afton's contributions to TV have long been forgotten.

We've had orchestra leader Joe Loss and former England

soccer captain Billy Wright making guest appearances—to judge a beauty contest and open a swimming pool. Just the kind of function they would attend in real life and bringing to *Crossroads* that authentic touch of reality for which we always strive.

Susan Denny, who now has her own programme on Capital Radio, one of the two London commercial radio stations, made some appearances for us ... as an English singer and dancer in a Paris night-club.

Susan used to work with me on *Lunch Box* so it was fun having her back in the studios again.

We also launched Sue Nicholls. I saw her in a BBC *Play of the Week* the other day and she has also been in *Dixon of Dock Green*.

When Sue started her TV career with us in the role of waitress Marilyn Gates she had a white wedding when she 'married' the Rev. Peter Hope, played by Neville Hughes.

Crossroads has a big following at hospitals and thirty women patients in Ward D1 of the Selly Oak Hospital signed a letter asking us to give her white satin bridal gown to a fellow patient—Irene McAndrew, eighteen, who was marrying a twenty-year-old carpenter, Adrian Price, at St Mary's Church, Wythall, near Birmingham.

Everyone at ATV was delighted with the idea, especially as Irene, an orphan, was the victim of a hereditary complaint that affects only one person in 500,000. Irene had been brought up in a children's home after the same disease had killed her mother and grandmother.

Normally the dress would have been ripped up and the material used for some other garment, but when we received the letter it was at once agreed to keep the gown intact so that it could be cleaned and despatched to the young bride.

Sue, daughter of Sir Harmar Nicholls, left us a couple of years later to further her career after winning a recording contract as a singer. Her departure happened quite by chance.

Tony Hatch, the composer and husband of Jackie Trent, who wrote our original *Crossroads* theme, wrote a number for Sue to sing in her role of the waitress Marilyn, who was then preparing for her first appearance as a night-club singer.

It was a soft love ballad called *Where will you be?* Louis Benjamin, managing director of the London Palladium who also runs Pye Records, was watching *Crossroads* and heard Sue sing the ballad. He liked the way she sang and, what's more, in the next few days he received enquiries from record dealers. We also, were receiving letters asking about the ballad and when could they hear it again.

By this time Sue had recorded the song for Pye and when she sang it again on the show it went into the Hit Parade. Cabaret engagements were offered, plus a Birmingham pantomime, so with this kind of career awaiting her Sue decided to leave us and branch out as a solo singer and actress.

It came as something of a shock when she handed in her notice but as none of the *Crossroads* cast is under long-term contract they can come and go as they wish.

Twenty-year-old Nadine Hanwell, till then a child actress on TV, took over from Sue in her first grown-up part.

It is incidents like these—and there have been scores of them—which distinguishes *Crossroads* from other TV serials, particularly *Coronation Street*.

In a real-life hotel, staff and guests are always changing and I'm sure that this is one of the main ingredients which has made our serial so popular with viewers since it enables new twists and turns in the various story lines. A new face must mean a new plot development. There is nothing static about *Crossroads* and this is especially true of Meg Richardson herself.

When *Crossroads* began, Meg, recently widowed, faced the task of making a new life for herself and her two young children. Now ten years later, she has built up her business and today, Meg is quite an affluent person. Meg's success has also been my success. We both have security and a way of life that we both enjoy.

As Meg I now have to have an extensive wardrobe—

women viewers would be quick to spot if I wore the same clothes too often.

But I still have two outfits in my TV wardrobe which go back to the start of *Crossroads*, ten years ago. They are both navy-blue dresses, one of my favourite colours. One is a navy serge with white collar and cuffs, and the other is a navy crêpe afternoon dress with organdie collar and matching cuffs.

I love these two dresses. You'll still see me wearing them from time to time and in fact, when John Bentley returned to the series, as Hugh Mortimer, he found Meg wearing the same dress she had worn the last time he had seen her—six years previously.

This of course, was quite deliberate.

They also have another attraction for me: I know that if I can still wear them I haven't put on any weight during the past ten years. So they're good for my ego in more ways than one.

My TV wardrobe is far more extensive than the one I have at home and there are times when Meg is far better dressed than Noele Gordon!

For a start, Meg has twenty two-piece suits, twenty evening gowns and up to thirty dresses. You would have to be very wealthy to have such a wardrobe, especially at today's prices.

To keep in fashion, all the dresses have three-inch hems; I hate to think how many times the girls in our Wardrobe Department have had to raise and lower these hem-lines since we've been on television.

None of Meg's clothes are, individually, very expensive— or at least, they haven't been. We pay £20 for a good off-the-peg dress and £30 for a suit. Summer frocks are in the £8–£10 range. But with prices soaring as they are, you'll have to forgive Meg if she seems to be wearing the same dress rather more often than she has done in the past.

When we go on location this means a complete new wardrobe, so I'm always pleased whenever it is possible for our unit to get away into the sunshine. Apart from the change in climate, it means new clothes too—and what woman could resist that?

One of our location visits was to Torremolinos in Spain and, at that time, we had actor Anthony Morton with us in the role of the Spanish chef, Carlos.

Actually, Tony wanted to play the role as an Italian, which he speaks fluently, but as the scriptwriters had written him in as a Spaniard he had to stay ... as a Spaniard. I never knew why.

On this occasion Reg Watson, our producer, had had the bright idea of moving the story away from our usual environment so that Meg could go with a few of the staff to Spain on holiday.

I was supposed to be staying at the villa of my wealthy boyfriend, Hugh Mortimer, and we rented a beautiful Moorish home for the occasion.

One sequence was supposed to show the return of Carlos to his native village. This was filmed in the square outside the white walled seventeenth-century Church of the Conception in the mimosa hung village of Mijas.

Eduardo Ariza, our handsome nineteen-year-old interpreter, looking like a young Ramon Navarro, explained to the local children how to greet the return of Carlos after his absence in England.

Carlos had to walk up and greet them with 'Chicos estoy de vuelta' which is Spanish for 'Children I am back'. But when our dashing Spaniard from *Crossroads* greeted them all in the hot sunshine, the children stopped playing and just looked at him as though he was a man from Mars.

Carlos was just as dumbfounded as they were.

'Golly,' he said, 'what's gone wrong? What *have* I said to them?'

But Eduardo reassured him.

'It's just that they know you aren't Spanish and that you haven't ever been here before,' he explained. 'They're puzzled.'

When we arrived, we were welcomed officially by

Malaga's Lord Mayor, Rafael Betes Ladron De Guevara. And in his best English, too.

Fifteen-stone Mr Morton listened to every word and every intonation. At the end, he looked very pleased with himself and I had to enquire why.

'Well, Nolly,' he said, 'as you know this is the first time I have ever been to Spain and in fact the first time I've ever heard a Spaniard trying to speak English. The Mayor is doing in real life what I have to do every day in the TV studio.

'Now that I've heard the real thing it's much better than any drama coach. I know now just what to do and Carlos will be more Spanish than he's ever been before.'

And he was, too.

On the Sunday some of the company went to a bullfight which, I must say, isn't exactly my idea of entertainment, so I stayed well away. As it happened, it turned out to be too much for eighteen-year-old Karen Shinwell, grand-daughter of Emanuel ('Manny') Shinwell, who had the role of a fourteen-year-old girl whom I had adopted—her first major TV booking.

Poor Karen had to leave the bullfight—in tears. It upset her so.

Everywhere we went in Spain we found the Spanish very helpful, and the British holidaymakers were astonished to find Meg Richardson in their midst, but of course, the Spaniards had no idea what it was all about and it was useless trying to explain.

They thought *Crossroads* was a British road sign and that we were there to study traffic problems!

We were once filming in Tunisia on location when a couple of holidaymakers came up to us and asked if they could join in. We pointed out that although we could do with some extras they had to be members of Equity.

'Oh, but we are,' they said. 'Both of us.'

It turned out that they were John Wade, the magician and his wife Elizabeth, who entertains at the piano.

John has made something like 300 radio and TV appearances and also worked on the David Nixon show for Thames TV as a magical adviser.

Once we knew they were 'pros', we were delighted to have them in a couple of scenes—and pay them too.

The small-part players in *Crossroads* are all Equity members. They get a special fee as crowd artists and many of them are old-time variety performers who have now retired.

Jack Hayes, once a well-known music hall comic, came to us in a small part. He did so well we built up his character of Enoch Jarvis and he was with us for quite a while before his death.

Bert Brownhill, famous as a pantomime dame, who used to have a variety act as a clippie standing at the back of the bus, on the platform and making cheeky remarks to the passengers, was another *Crossroads* regular. He had the role of Sir Henry Barker, a well-to-do industrialist who turned up at our motel in his Rolls-Royce for an army reunion.

Norah Blaney, who was a top-of-the-bill performer with Gwen Farrar, was also with us as the novelist Miss Leopold.

Ian Patterson, the Scottish actor who was in the Broadway production of *Oh, What a Lovely War*, has also done his *Crossroads* stint as my brother Andy.

Ian has a degree in engineering, but he decided on a theatrical career after winning a scholarship to study singing in Vienna for two years.

Jan Butlin came to us for twelve episodes but she spent the whole time in bed: as Joyce Hepworth, an air hostess who had sprained her ankle and couldn't move.

'I don't mind,' she said, 'it's really rather restful.'

CHAPTER THREE

Crossroads was developed in a curious way.

Apart from Granada's *Coronation Street,* the only other serial on the air at that time was the BBC's *Compact*, both twice-weeklies.

Once it had been decided to provide a *daily* programme built around me as an actress instead of a TV personality, Sir Lew Grade set about finding the writers.

He could hardly approach the *Coronation Street* team so—as I've already mentioned—he contacted the partnership of Peter Ling and Hazel Adair, the BBC's scriptwriting team who had devised and written *Compact*, the story of a lush woman's magazine, which had a big following on BBC TV.

By this time, Sir Lew had already received another programme format from someone else but when he outlined this to Peter and Hazel and offered them a six-months' contract to edit and shape the new serial for him they turned down his offer.

'We're not working on someone else's idea,' said Peter. 'We'd rather work on our own.'

Their meeting with Sir Lew was on a Friday. He told them to return with their proposition on the following Monday.

After working over the week-end, they were back on Monday morning with a two-page format based on the adventures of two families living in the Midlands—widowed Meg Richardson and her married sister Kitty Jarvis.

Peter and Hazel had chosen the name Meg for me, quite unaware that I had had my biggest stage success as another Meg—Meg Brockie—in the stage musical *Brigadoon.*

So Meg has brought me luck—twice. The first of many strange coincidences in *Crossroads*.

Compact, which started in January 1962, had been running on BBC TV for nearly three years but within six months of *Crossroads* starting, the BBC dropped *Compact* and brought in a new twice-weekly serial *96, Park Lane*. The newcomer never had much of an impact however, and it was soon dropped.

'*Crossroads* helped to kill them both off,' admits Peter Ling and he has been associated with our success ever since.

After their meeting with Sir Lew Grade, Peter and Hazel then went to work in the Earl's Court flat they rented as an office. First they had to work out a story line based on their original synopsis, rather like a short story, to cover the first six weeks' episodes.

Then this overall story itself, covering ten foolscap pages, had to be adapted into daily short stories for each daily episode. Finally, these were turned into TV scripts of short two-minute scenes.

This same system operates today. Story lines are planned three months ahead, although last year *Crossroads* was planned till the end of 1974. This was arranged as long ago as the previous March, when Reg Watson left to take up his new post with Australian TV.

Peter Ling is the all-important Storyliner. He is the one who provides the plots without which *Crossroads* could never come to life. He worked with Hazel Adair for the first three years and then continued on his own when Hazel moved into the production and writing of feature films, thus ending an eight years' partnership which began when they met in 1950 while working on the children's series *Whirligig* for the BBC.

Their original story line was centred on the reasonably affluent life of Meg Richardson who was turning her Georgian home into a motel and her sister, Kitty Jarvis, living in a seedy back street on the outskirts of industrial Birmingham.

The jealousy and envy that Kitty felt for her sister and

Meg's reactions were to be the pivot of the whole situation and the basic story would have been about the clash between the two sisters.

This was the outline first put before Sir Lew and this was what he bought. I often wonder if he has ever noticed he didn't quite get what he ordered. For when it came to putting the show on the screen, the two characters of Kitty and Meg—as portrayed by Beryl Johnstone and myself—turned out so much nicer than anyone expected.

If jealousy had been introduced and a clash in temperaments developed, no one would have believed us. In other words, the viewers liked us both from the start so we couldn't just be turned into quarrelsome women. When, sadly, Beryl died, the whole story line had to be changed.

Beryl Johnstone's untimely death naturally presented a problem for our writers, for it meant Kitty Jarvis had to die too. We could have made this a great, emotional event—with a village funeral; Meg in mourning and everyone in tears, but this would have seemed completely out of place since Beryl really *had* died and all our viewers knew it.

On the other hand, we could have sent Kitty off to California or somewhere. It would have taken her out of the serial, but as far as the viewers were concerned, she would still be alive.

This too, seemed wrong for all the obvious reasons.

Eventually, Reg hit on the solution. Kitty was kept out of the serial for another two weeks and then, in the village post office, Miss Tatum just remarked casually to a customer 'Wasn't it sad about Kitty Jarvis?'

The other woman replied 'Yes, we're all going to miss her very much.' No further reference was ever made.

Peter Ling now comes to Birmingham every other Tuesday to attend a production conference held by Jack Barton, who has taken over as producer in place of Reg Watson. Also in attendance—Margaret French, our production manager, plus the four writers and three directors who put the serial together on the studio floor.

At these meetings, they discuss the two weeks of daily

story lines already submitted by Peter a fortnight previously. Casting is discussed—which actors would be best for any new roles and there also takes place an unusual procedure which is unique in British television.

This is the 'casting' of the writers. For, over the years, we have used some seventy writers. Peter Ling and our production office know their various characteristics and we have a system, started by Reg Watson, in which various scriptwriters are given individual stories, best suited for them to develop.

The customary method in TV scriptwriting is quite different. Normally a writer is given a script to write and he does the whole job himself—or in collaboration with others. But in *Crossroads* we have five or six story lines running at the same time, so each of our writers works on his own story, with his own characters, without concerning himself as to what is happening to the rest of the *Crossroads* folk.

We have specialized scriptwriters, too. Ivor Jay is an expert on the Black Country; Michala Crees is very good at comedy. This is why, at the end of *Crossroads*, you will see the names of four writers—but they haven't sat down and written the show together—just individual segments which, when pieced together, make up the whole programme.

Crossroads writers receive a three months' contract to work on the serial, and during this period, each of them writes some 120 scenes of about two minutes.

Our system of assigning writers to story lines is quite new. I'm sure this fresh approach has paid off in the many different subjects we're able to cover and the different situations which arise.

Peter Ling writes out all his stories for us in long hand, to be typed by his secretary, at his terrace house in Hastings, Sussex. In between his *Crossroads* commitments, he is also one of the four writers working on the BBC's radio serial *Waggoner's Walk*.

He has four children and tells a very touching *Crossroads* story involving his eldest daughter.

Eighteen-year-old Vicky, a student, used to make fun of

Crossroads and all the many twists and turns that her father has invented for us over the years. As a modern young girl, she considered we served no useful purpose, preferring BBC-2 programmes to anything *Crossroads* could offer. But an incident on Hastings pier caused her to change her mind.

The Ling family were on the pier with some friends, when Peter went across to get some small change from the elderly woman attendant.

'Excuse me,' she said, 'but someone said you are the gentleman who writes *Crossroads*.'

Peter agreed that he was.

'In that case,' she said, 'may I just thank you for the great happiness you have brought me over the years. I am a widow and live by myself. I have no family and I get very lonely, but every day I watch *Crossroads*. I live with Meg and all the others. They have become part of my life, my family.'

Vicky took her father's arm as they walked away.

'Daddy,' she told him, 'I'll never laugh at *Crossroads* again.'

This story of the woman on Hasting pier is typical of the people to whom *Crossroads* has become a way of life, and who follow our adventures regularly on the small screen. They turn up in the most surprising and unexpected places.

For example, councillors of Farndon, Nottinghamshire, agreed to switch the time of their meetings so as to enable their clerk to watch his favourite TV programme—*Crossroads*.

They had decided to meet at 7 p.m. instead of 7.30 until their clerk, Mr Percy Staveley, pointed out that our programme did not finish in their area till 6.55 p.m. Further, as it took him a quarter of an hour to get from his home to the meeting in the village hall, he would be missing the last fifteen minutes of the programme every time there was a council meeting.

The councillors saw his point at once—especially as some of them were also *Crossroads* fans. So they agreed to start their meetings ten minutes later to enable Mr Staveley to stay at home a little longer and see the whole programme.

'I'm very grateful to the councillors,' said Mr Staveley. 'I find the programme very interesting and as I've been following it for four years, I wouldn't like to miss it.'

We also know that the Queen and members of the Royal Family watch us sometimes at Buckingham Palace. I learned this from Prince Philip when he visited the studios while we were at work on a *Crossroads* episode.

On this particular afternoon, I was involved in a scene with Maggie Hanley—widow of Jimmy Hanley who used to be with us. Maggie had dressed herself up as a tart—all part of the plot—to visit the motel.

'Who is she supposed to be?' enquired Prince Philip.

Well, as you can imagine, I didn't quite know what to say. I didn't like to use the word tart. Somehow I felt it wasn't the right expression for Royalty.

'Well,' I stammered, 'as a matter of fact she's really a woman police officer who is supposed to be making discreet undercover enquiries at the motel.'

'Then why is she dressed like that?' persisted Prince Philip.

'Well, that's just it. You see she's in disguise so that no one will think she's a policewoman.'

'I see. But why those extraordinary clothes? Who on earth goes about like that? Who is she supposed to be?'

I decided there was nothing for it but to tell the truth.

'She's supposed to be playing a lady of easy virtue, but I didn't like to tell you so.'

'Why ever not?' laughed the Duke. 'I know what they are, you know!'

On another occasion we had a visit from Princess Alexandra. On this particular day all the performers on the set happened to be women. The Princess asked me what scene we were shooting and I gave her a rough outline of the current plot.

'*Crossroads* does seem to be something of a matriarchy,' she commented. 'Don't you think so, Miss Gordon?'

'Yes, Ma'am,' I said. 'It is at the moment.'

'What are you going to do in this scene?' asked the Royal visitor.

'Nothing much,' I said. 'Something awful has just happened to my son and I just have to faint.'

The Princess was most intrigued.

'You mean actually fall down in a heap?'

'Yes.'

'But how can you do that without hurting yourself?'

'Oh,' I replied, 'it isn't difficult. They teach us that at drama school.'

'Show me,' said the Princess, with a twinkle.

So I did. I just fell. Just where I was—right at her feet.

'You make it look very easy,' said the Princess.

The studio hands gave me a polite round of applause and, as our local ATV news camera team were covering the Royal visit, the whole incident appeared in our Midlands News Bulletin that same evening—but without the sound track of our conversation and no real explanation of what it was all about.

I had forgotten the incident, but a couple of days later I pulled up at my usual garage for some petrol.

'I saw you on the telly,' said the attendant. 'That really was a terrible thing to do. Fancy falling down drunk in front of Royalty.'

I'm sure he still believes I was ...

Tony Blackburn, the BBC disc-jockey, is one of our regular followers. Whenever he and his actress wife have to miss one of our programmes he arranges for that particular edition to be recorded on his videotape machine so that he can play it back and see what he has missed.

Mrs Mary Wilson also watches us from time to time. During her husband's previous term of office when she was living in Downing Street, scores of letters arrived at No. 10 asking her to intervene when *Crossroads* was dropped by Thames Television in the London area.

Now although I am very flattered and appreciate the loyalty of these viewers, this really wasn't a matter with which I would expect the Prime Minister's wife to become personally involved.

However it so happened that Mrs Wilson found herself attending a film premiere with Mr Harold Wilson, and among the other guests was Lord Aylestone, Chairman of the Independent Broadcasting Authority which controls commercial television. Mrs Wilson mentioned to Lord Aylestone that she had received all these letters and jokingly asked him if he could do anything to persuade Thames Television to bring back *Crossroads*.

Lord Aylestone pointed out that he could not interfere with an internal programme decision by any particular company but he promised to pass on the complaints to the programme executives at Thames Television.

'We've had a lot of protests over this at the Authority, as well,' he said.

As you might expect, the company responsible for dropping *Crossroads* from its schedules had also received hundreds of letters from disappointed fans asking for it to be reinstated. There had been phone calls too. On the first night the programme was dropped, the switchboard was jammed with angry viewers and this continued for several subsequent evenings.

Finally, Brian Tesler, who was then Programme Controller for Thames Television, gave way. The public won and *Crossroads* was put back at the exact moment in the plot at which it had been dropped.

This explains why Londoners always see a different edition to the rest of the country. They are in fact, six months behind. Originally, when Yorkshire TV first came on the air, they too were opposed to *Crossroads* and decided against screening but so many Yorkshire viewers kept asking for the serial that the company later capitulated and *Crossroads* has been on Yorkshire TV ever since.

Granada, as I have already told you, joined in two years ago when commercial television started full-scale afternoon TV for the first time. But for some reason, they decided to start off with sequences which we had shown over a year

45

before. So although London is six months behind us, Lancashire lags further still—fourteen months.

Incidentally, when we in *Crossroads* heard of Mrs Wilson's remark to Lord Aylestone we decided that, joke or not, something had to be done by way of thanking her. So we all signed a nice presentation card for her and sent it off to Downing Street, adding that we had reserved a chalet for her at our motel and she would be welcome any time.

The hallmark of our success is that most of the public believe we really are the characters we play on the screen. I've already told how some of the cast get assaulted in the street for mean or despicable actions which those ingenious *Crossroads* writers call on them to perform from time to time.

In my own case I'm always the suffering one—it's sympathy that I get for the way life has treated me. But I'm not complaining. It's better to have love and sympathy from everyone—than hate.

Few people seem to think of me as an actress any more. Everyone assumes I'm in the hotel business. When I go into a restaurant, the manager always likes to show me round the kitchens and, if it's an hotel, he talks to me as though I was a member of the Hotel and Catering Association.

I even get invitations to talk to caterers at their conventions. I don't mind going along but I have to tell them, right from the start, that I'm no real hotel-keeper. I know nothing about catering and although I'm a reasonable cook I'm not in the *Cordon Bleu* class.

Crossroads actually has a big following in the catering world. It's screened just before restaurant staff leave home to get ready for their evening shift. As we have a catering and hotel background their interest is understandable, and we have a professional catering expert and hotel owner who sees that no mistakes are made in this sphere. He is Geoffrey Lancashire, who owns the Chasedale Hotel at Ross-on-Wye.

Geoffrey, and his wife Edna, have been friends of mine

46

for years and they have given us valuable advice and assistance ever since we opened our TV motel. The Lancashires have been our unofficial advisers throughout. We send them scripts to check whenever we have problems on the hotel and catering side and I have been able to model much of Meg's expertise as an hotel owner on Edna Lancashire.

We must be doing a good job; Carlos, our original Spanish chef, played by Anthony Morton, once had an enquiry from the Birmingham branch of the Women's Voluntary Services asking him to quote for supplying two hundred dinners a day. Another time, a chef at Rackhams, the Birmingham store, wrote in for a job in our kitchen.

Sometimes this insistence on accuracy gets us into hot water.

In one episode we had a councillor asking a young couple for a bribe in return for helping them to get a council house. This is not unknown in the municipal world and there have been several court cases and convictions for similar offences. After all, if *Crossroads* is to reflect life—which it does—then the seamy side must be shown as well. It may even act as a deterrent to other councillors who might be tempted in this way.

However, our serial is produced in Birmingham and this particular twist in the plot was rather too much for some members of the Birmingham City Council.

Alderman Harry Watton called us 'pig-swill entertainment' at a Council meeting. Another member of the council, Mr Geoffrey Austin, said that as it was widely accepted that *Crossroads* was based on the City of Birmingham (which it isn't), the suggestion that a councillor would ask for money under these circumstances was 'an imputation against the chairman, members and officers of the Birmingham Public Works Committee.'

This is, of course, the committee which is responsible for rehousing Birmingham families who have lost their homes under compulsory purchase orders.

The City's Lord Mayor at the time, Alderman George

Barrow, said that he too, deplored the episode but it was obvious that no legal action could be taken.

However, we did have some supporters—and Mrs Nora Hinks asked if the council, in addition to its other duties, would be taking on the job of vetting our TV programmes!

I have only told this story to illustrate the tremendous impact which our programme has and the great care that has to be taken to be accurate and fair-minded in the presentation of topical subjects.

No one, surely, is going to assume that the Birmingham Public Works Committee has corrupt councillors just because we featured one in a fictional series on television. I wouldn't have thought so. But on the other hand, as recent events have shown, there *is* corruption in parts of the building and development community.

Birmingham City Council are not the only ones to claim to have suffered at the hands of *Crossroads* scriptwriters. In one sequence these inventive creators sent me to jail and had me appearing in drab, grey prison garb, scrubbing floors and being locked up in a cell every night.

It all happened because, in one plot, I was found to be driving with a defective tyre; I braked on an icy road to avoid a cat and hit Vince Parker (Peter Brookes) who was riding his motor cycle. It could have been manslaughter but instead, for some while it was touch and go as to whether Vince would lose his sight.

Meg was breathalysed but the test proved negative and she was charged with dangerous driving and having a defective tyre.

In law, of course, she should not have braked to avoid an animal and there is no defence to driving with a threadbare tyre. You can be sent to prison in similar circumstances in real life and the whole idea of this particular story line was to show how an ordinary, respectable person can get into serious trouble through this type of motoring offence.

Meg received a month's jail sentence. She was so distraught at the thought that she had blinded Vince that she would not agree to appeal, preferring to serve her sentence.

However, she was later persuaded to do so and as she was a first offender, her appeal was upheld and she only served a fortnight behind bars.

Reg Watson and his production team took expert advice throughout to ensure both the court and prison scenes were authentic. We had the help of police and probation officers and they visited Winson Green prison with Rex Spencer, our Head of Design, to make sure our prison sequences looked like the real thing.

Maybe they were too accurate. For although it's a male prison, for Midlanders there is only one jail ... Winson Green.

As soon as Meg had been locked up in her cell for the night, viewers were on the phone—not to the ATV studios but to Winson jail itself.

They jammed the switchboard—asking if they could send flowers and books; what were the visiting days; would Meg get time off for good behaviour and similar questions.

The next day gifts and letters started to arrive; there were more phone calls. Finally the Governor of Winson Green jail came on the phone to Reg Watson.

'You've got to help us,' he said. 'We're getting so many calls about Meg Richardson, we can't get on with our work.'

So we then gave the prison switchboard a special phone number at ATV to which they referred all enquiries about Meg.

For the next two weeks we had a girl on duty who did nothing else but answer their queries and reassure them that Meg Richardson wasn't really in a cell at Winson Green but was alive and well and living her normal life as Noele Gordon.

The entire motoring sequence was prepared in consultation with legal experts and this careful planning and preparation goes into all our stories.

When it was decided to involve my son Sandy (Roger Tonge) in a car crash, Reg Watson and Peter Ling spent two days at Stoke Mandeville Hospital to obtain general information and background material. They were given every assistance by the medical staff and were able to talk to patients who are themselves living the lives of paraplegics ... as Sandy now does.

We have had many hospital scenes over the years and they are always carefully planned and researched beforehand with the co-operation of hospitals and our own medical advisers.

At one time we had Jane Mortimer killed off through a brain operation. This role was played by Rosalie Ashley, who used to be a well-known TV hostess for the BBC and is now the wife of Raymond, the hair-stylist of Teazy Weazy fame. As Rosalie didn't want to be tied down to a long run she was the ideal choice for this part.

Incidentally, Raymond has also appeared in *Crossroads*. He played his own real-life role of a hair stylist, but we called him Monsieur Fabrice and he showed off some hair fashions in Vera Downend's salon.

As Raymond himself admits, it was TV which brought him national fame back in the fifties in the days of the BBC monopoly. A few appearances in Richard Afton's variety series *Quite Contrary* doing hair styles and Raymond became a national figure. Indeed, on the strength of television, he branched out of the West End and set up his very successful chain of hairdressing salons throughout the country.

'Television made it all possible,' he says.

So it seemed appropriate, when we needed a sequence involving hair styling to engage Raymond.

This is another unusual aspect of the way *Crossroads* is put together, although it is not unknown in the USA. Just as in America's *Hawaii Five-O*, we employ real life people in their own roles whenever we can, though of course, they have to be members of Equity.

Hawaii Five-O, shot on location, always has professional actors and actresses for the main roles but the bank managers, hotel assistants, shoppers and others are all genuine folk employed in these occupations in real life.

Wherever possible, we do the same.

For one sequence we wanted a magician so we called in Clifford Davis, Television Editor of the *Daily Mirror* who is also a member of Equity and a professional magician.

We already had an actor (Alan Haines) playing a wayward, rascally, down-at-heel wizard, but we wanted some real magic on the show to give a genuine touch.

Clifford was asked if he could levitate Sue Hanson, who plays Diane, the waitress.

'No problem,' he said and told Reg Watson just what he needed to pull off this feat. But of course Clifford was thinking in terms of a stage illusion. It all sounded terribly complicated so, in the end, it was decided to use the magic of television itself—in other words, trick camera work.

For a start we were supposed to have a magician's convention at the hotel—a handful of local Birmingham conjurors were engaged to stand around performing tricks. Clifford Davis gave a little show himself and then Alan Haines took over as the rascally illusionist.

He stood in front of Sue and got her to lie down on a plank balanced between two chairs.

'All set?' he asked her.

'Fine,' she said.

Then, slowly, Sue was levitated. She rose a good nine feet above the ground. But did she? I'll let you into a secret and as it's TV magic and not about a real professional stage illusion, I don't suppose the Magic Circle will really mind. The *Crossroads* levitation really did baffle millions. Now for the first time, here's how it was done.

Clifford Davis and Reg Watson worked out a way to make Sue appear to rise on the screen although, in fact, she never actually moved.

Two cameras were used. The first camera was fixed on the plank with the two chairs at either end. The second camera was fixed on Sue herself. She was lying fully stretched on top of a pedestal covered in black velvet—the same black velvet that had been used to hang behind the plank and the chairs.

51

So, since the two velvet drapes matched exactly, you couldn't tell one from the other. This was important.

The technicians then had to line up the two pictures on the two cameras. The picture which showed Sue lying full-length was then superimposed on the picture of the empty plank. By fitting the one on the other exactly, it looked on the screen as though Sue really was lying on the plank.

Then, at the word of command, Sue slowly rose without any visible means of support.

But all that had really happened was that the first camera (which covered her stretched full length) was slowly moved upwards and, as the camera went up, so Sue appeared to rise as well.

When the first camera stopped—there she was ... levitated.

Naturally we were all kept out of the studio while this was going on and only essential performers, plus the technicians involved, were allowed to see just how it was done.

This levitation illusion caused something of a sensation and this is the first time that I have told anyone how it was actually done.

Just before Clifford came to bring Sue down to earth he put his hand above his head, as if to give her a little pat. By looking in the studio monitor, which was showing the superimposed picture that viewers would see, he was able to make it appear as though he was actually touching her.

At a given signal, Sue gave a little jump and a squeak so that as far as 14,000,000 viewers were concerned, she really had been levitated and was stretched horizontally above the magician's head.

Finally, to close this episode, producer Reg decided on a laugh. He had Clifford levitate Amy Turtle (Ann George) and there she was hanging in mid-air above our heads as the *Crossroads* theme faded us all from the screen.

The same electronic method was used.

We've even had a chimp on the show—Tina, one of the famous chimps from those TV tea advertisements.

For our purposes, however, Tina had to become Bugs.

52

She was part of a variety act supposed to be staying in the motel.

The three-year-old chimp was a great hit. She is one of thirteen kept by Miss Molly Badham at the Twycross Zoo, near Atherstone, Warwickshire, so this makes Tina a Midlands performer. And after all, we always try to use local talent whenever we can.

It's Tina who gets up to most of those tricks in the TV commercials—Miss Badham brought her along to the studios for, she told us, Tina is by far the cleverest of them all. She caused a bit of havoc in the studios but no more really than some of our more temperamental human performers!

We also used a camel for some sequences. I don't know what her name was in Arabic but we called her Lotus.

Lotus came into the story when we were on location at Djerba, 360 miles across the desert from Tunis. We had gone there to film sequences for a make-believe Tunisian hotel 'The Desert Coral' which we introduced as a background to the serial after the original *Crossroads* motel had been blown up and a new one was being built in the Midlands.

Thousands of outside shots were filmed against a background of doomed villas, Arab bazaars, and flowering pomegranates. Five of the island's hotels were used to provide exteriors and then these were used with interior scenes which were put together in ATV's Birmingham studios.

A great deal of background research had to be done beforehand so Hazel Adair went out to Djerba ahead of us and she asked so many questions that the local Secret Police started making enquiries about her.

When *Crossroads* started we were often criticized for our so-called cardboard situations and plots, but the truth is, ten years ago this is just what viewers demanded of a daily TV serial. They wanted cardboard; they wanted escapisms; they didn't expect anything more of television than plastic plots having little or nothing to do with present-day life.

But as viewers' tastes have changed and become more adult, so *Crossroads* has changed too.

There was quite an outcry when we first had a story about an unmarried mother, a girl who came to work for me as a waitress and had a child by a merchant seaman. Since then, we have had two illegitimate children born to young girls and there have been no protests from anyone.

Viewers today expect realistic situations and our plots deal more and more with contemporary life. But at the same time, we are very conscious that what is seen and accepted in a family sitting-room, is very different to the dialogue and situations you would be prepared to accept in a stage play or in a cinema.

So although *Crossroads* handles subjects like alcoholism, witchcraft, women in prison, abortion, vandalism, and the physically handicapped, there is always the knowledge that such situations and dialogue must be presented in a way that we know will be acceptable to family viewers.

For one thing, I don't suppose many people realize this, but you will never find any actor or actress smoking a cigarette during a *Crossroads* episode ... pipes or a cigar, maybe. But never a cigarette.

This is because the Independent Broadcasting Authority instructed us not to do so from the first programme. In addition, some while ago the IBA, in the interests of national health, banned all cigarette advertisements from the screen.

The loss in advertising revenue for the ITV companies has run into millions. But the IBA rule 'No cigarette smoking before seven p.m.' was in existence long before the advertising ban and this is why you never see Meg with a cigarette—but you'll often see Noele Gordon.

Away from the screen, I must confess, I am a heavy smoker. It's always a strain to carry through the day's shooting of a couple of *Crossroads* episodes without a single cigarette—at least before the cameras.

It's really rather odd. Meg is a non-smoker but I am just

the opposite. I only wish I had the same will power as Meg —and so does my mother. But I'm sorry to say, it's really too late for me to change.

However, there was one occasion when the Authority permitted someone to smoke on *Crossroads* in the interests of realism.

Raymond Mason had the role of an alcoholic who had to make a suicide attempt by jumping under a train. In the few moments while the man sought the courage to run across the railway track, he was obviously in a state of high nervous tension.

It was only natural that a man in such a situation would want to smoke and, from an actor's point of view, it would have been much harder to register such tense strain without lighting a cigarette with a shaky hand and puffing away nervously before stubbing it out—and going to face Eternity.

Under these circumstances, the Authority lifted its ban and Raymond Mason was allowed to smoke!

The suicide attempt was filmed at Tysley sidings, which is on the outskirts of Birmingham and about five miles from our studios.

British Rail were happy to provide the train and the facilities in return for a payment of £15. As the site was on the main line, the only suitable time for the filming was on a Sunday when there were fewer trains.

Everything went as planned at the first run-through except that there was a woman with a baby and a pram, watching the whole incident from the railway bridge overhead. And her presence just couldn't be explained away in the plot!

By this time, of course, the so-called express which we had hired for the occasion had vanished into the distance leaving our film unit there—but no trains.

The situation was explained to the British Rail foreman in charge and he suggested that we should film the incident again, but, this time, using a *real* express.

'After all,' he said, 'you're only going to show your actor

running towards the train—the rest will be left to the viewer's imagination.'

And this is what we did do. The foreman martialled twenty men to line the track and signal with 'thumbs up' signs to the next express train driver that he wasn't to worry if he saw a man run down the embankment.

Somehow or other, when the next train *did* approach, the driver got the message—and carried on.

Raymond Mason ran down the slope. There was no woman and child watching from the bridge. The express rushed past. And viewers had the impression that a suicide attempt really *had* taken place.

It probably looked even more realistic with a real express thundering by with its long line of carriages and faces at the windows.

I've often wondered if the train driver and his passengers ever saw that particular episode of *Crossroads* and recognized themselves.

They must have been surprised if they did.

CHAPTER FOUR

I always knew I was going to be an actress and I always hoped I would be a star. It was Mother who kept telling me so and it was she who had the faith and confidence in me to ensure it all happened.

As you can guess from my christian name, I was born on Christmas Day—just as Sir Lew Grade, my boss at ATV.

My mother's guidance and help throughout my career is typical of our family for we have always had this strong matriarchal strain. In fact, Meg Richardson would make an ideal Gordon, for her character and ability to cope is typical of the women from whom I am descended.

My great-grandmother must have been a wonderful woman for she owned a shipping line of sailing vessels, based at Macduff, Bannshire, which she inherited after her husband, who used to trade with Czarist Russia, was killed in a sleigh accident at Ormsk.

She travelled to Russia to bring back his body for burial in Scotland; a very hazardous adventure for a woman on her own in those days.

She continued to run the shipping line herself, just as Meg—also widowed—first started *Crossroads* as a motel.

My grandmother married a ship's captain in the days when everything was still sail and my grandfather was based in Baltimore working for an American shipping line. She saw very little of him and, in fact, he spent so much time in the USA he even took out American citizenship.

Mother also married a seafaring man, a Scottish ship's engineer, but I never really knew him. He was mostly at sea when I was a youngster, sailing to Australia and back. He would spend three months at sea and three weeks at home.

The sea has been in my blood for generations and I'm sure if I'd been born a man I would have been a sailor, but I don't fancy life as a ship's stewardess and that's about the only job afloat for a woman.

As an only child, it was left to my mother to bring me up —in a strict, Scots Presbyterian atmosphere I must add.

Till recently we lived together in a large Georgian house called Weir End at Ross-on-Wye, but I also had to have a flat in Birmingham to be near the studios and this meant I only saw Mother at week-ends.

I didn't really like the idea of her being in such a large house alone during the week, so now we have both moved back to Birmingham and have adjoining flats. This means I can keep an eye on her though, more often, she is keeping an eye on me!

I have a nickname for her—Jockey—and this is what everyone calls her round the ATV studios. I don't really know why this became her nickname—perhaps it's because she's rather small.

She stood in the wings when I first sang in public and she has been there ever since. It was Jockey who groomed me for my stage career; she had always felt she herself, would have liked to be in show business but as she is essentially a shy person, she never found the courage to do anything about it. But she was determined not only to put me on the stage but also to ensure I became a success. Thanks to Jockey, it all came true.

I've always had a good memory—which is why I don't have much trouble in learning lines—and I can remember Mother and I living at 139 Clements Road, East Ham, when I wasn't much more than two years old.

We had a typical, suburban house with a paved garden in the front and a small garden at the back. I remember Mother's big double bed, a beautiful piece of furniture with brass knobs and rails. Unfortunately, when we moved, she gave it away and I have often wished she had kept it. How splendid it would have looked in my flat today, or even on the set of *Crossroads*. Mother's old brass bedstead has become very fashionable and the genuine Victorian article is now in such short suply that firms are copying them and doing a fine business.

My first stage appearance was at the old East Ham Palace, a well-known music hall, when I was a pupil at the Maude Wells Dancing Academy. Mother had covered my face in strawberry jam and given me a jam jar to carry for a charity concert. I had to sing *Dear Little Jammy Face* and I remember I enjoyed every moment of it. I was two and a half!

The following year, they even let me dress up as a comedy clergyman, a censored version of George Robey's Minister of Mirth act, but unlike Mr Robey, I didn't tell any jokes, I just had to sing a comic song. So I really did start young.

When I first went to school I had a marked Scots accent and all the other girls used to tease me, but I soon lost it and now only Mother retains her North of the Border brogue.

We lived at Westcliff for a while and then moved back to Ilford. By this time I was a teenager and I was taken away from school and sent to study drama at the Royal Academy of Dramatic Art. We hadn't a great deal of money but I was tested by Sir Kenneth Barnes and when he accepted me as a fifteen-year-old pupil, it was my mother who persuaded my father to let me enrol. The fees were sixteen guineas a term—quite a lot in those days.

At the Academy they taught us everything there is to know about acting. I played in Shakespeare, Shaw, and all the classics. One term I was cast as Eliza Doolittle in *Pygmalion*. It was wonderful training for me.

It was while I was still at RADA that I got my first professional job—as an understudy in the comedy *Aren't Men Beasts?* at the Strand Theatre.

John Mills, now one of our foremost straight actors, who made his TV début in the ATV series *Zoo Gang* last year, was one of the stars. In those days he was a handsome, juvenile lead, having progressed from the chorus of musical comedies.

Robertson Hare and Alfred Drayton were the comedians and there were four main roles for women. I had the job of a walking understudy, which meant that I had to understudy all four of them. It so happened that each of them in turn caught chickenpox and as each one left the cast I stepped in and took their place, so I finished up by playing all four roles in my first West End engagement.

Leaving RADA, I got a job with a repertory company in Edinburgh and then I came back to London and auditioned for a part in Eugene O'Neill's drama *Ah Wilderness* at the King's Theatre, Hammersmith.

This particular production was also televised by the BBC from their old Alexandra Palace studios—the first big drama ever seen on British television. The year was 1937.

I had the part of a maid and as there were no recording facilities in those days, everything had to be televised live and non-stop, exactly as it happened.

This was live television with a vengeance. The play's action filled three studios and after finishing in one scene everyone had to rush down the corridor to be ready for the next sequence in another studio. Good training for *Crossroads*—although, of course, I never realized it at the time.

The cameras were also very antiquated by today's standards and required much more studio lighting than today. The heat generated by the arc lamps was really fierce and the longer you stayed in front of the cameras the hotter you became. During this BBC-TV production of *Ah Wilderness* the heat became so intense that our make-up started to run down our faces and I was forced to drop a silver tray I was holding, for the heat was burning my fingers.

There weren't many television sets around in those days and there probably weren't enough viewers around to notice, but after putting on the play on Saturday evening, everything had to be repeated again the following Thursday —live.

A year later I was working with Harry Hanson's Court

Players, another repertory company at the old Penge Empire in South London. One of my favourite roles was Sadie Thompson in Somerset Maugham's *Rain* and it was during this that John Logie Baird, the television pioneer, sent one of his assistants backstage one night to invite me to take part in some colour TV experiments at the nearby Crystal Palace studios, site of the IBA and BBC transmitters today.

Baird probably asked me not only because of my black hair and blue eyes, but also because Penge happened to be the closest theatre to his laboratories.

He used to send his Rolls-Royce to pick me up at the stage-door and take me to his studio where I sat in front of a colour TV camera while technicians tried out various effects.

'You're the first actress in the world to be seen on colour television,' Baird told me.

I spent a whole summer visiting his studios twice a week and I also took part in his big screen TV experiments in a Tottenham Court Road cinema.

I could see myself on colour TV monitors and it was all very lifelike, though not as realistic as today. Baird's experiments were all done over closed circuit and his system, although mechanical, was a tremendous breakthrough despite the fact that it was later discarded for the electronic method we use today.

It was while I was at the Penge Empire that I got my first big break. In one of the plays, *Suspect*, I had to sing a number which, in itself, was unusual for a straight play but was all part of the plot.

We changed the plays every week and it so happened that during the week in which I was singing this one song in *Suspect*, George Black, then managing director of the London Palladium, whose sons were later to start Tyne Tees Television, was in the audience.

Until then, I had only been known as a straight actress in various small repertory companies, but Mr Black was so impressed that he put me on tour in a musical that he had produced and which had been a big hit at the old London Hippodrome, now the theatre-restaurant Talk of the Town.

The revue was *Black Velvet* and although I was a principal I was hardly a star. I was paid £10 a week. It was *Black Velvet* which launched me into the musical side of the theatre and I stayed in musical plays and revues right through to my *Lunch Box* days on Midlands television.

I left *Black Velvet* for a while—and for a very special reason as I will tell you later. But I later returned and when the tour finally finished after two years I found myself a job in a West End musical *Let's Face It* with Bobbie Howes, father of Sally Ann Howes. When Joyce Barbour fell ill, I took over as leading lady.

Lisbon Story at the London Hippodrome followed (I was also in the film version); a spell with ENSA entertaining the Services; Prince Charming at the Alexandra Theatre, Birmingham, and then, the following year, back at the Alex again but as Dick Whittington this time. I was also in the A. P. Herbert musical *Big Ben* presented by C. B. Cochran at the Adelphi Theatre in the Strand and soon after this came my biggest break of all ... *Brigadoon*.

This was the show that really established me, the show that made me a West End star.

My agent had seen the original production in New York and he felt sure that I would be ideal for a certain role.

'It's small, but important,' he said. 'You could make it a show stopper.'

Brigadoon, based on a German folk-story, tells of a forgotten village in the Scottish highlands which, once every one hundred years, comes to life. The essence of the tale is that if you believe in something deeply enough, then it will happen—even a miracle.

The part I was after was a saucy one—not a bit like Meg Richardson. To put it bluntly, I was the village tart.

The auditions would not be held for at least another six months so I turned down all other offers at much more money and went back to work in various local London repertory companies—just to earn a few pounds to keep myself and ensure that I would be available when they started casting.

I was after the part of the skittish young Scots girl who had two rather special light comedy songs to sing, *The Love of My Life* and *My Mother's Wedding Day*. I had the music flown over from New York and I spent every moment of my spare time not only learning the songs, but learning how to put over the somewhat risqué lyrics, how to get laughs and a sense of fun from the ballads as well as sing them.

When the time came for the auditions at Her Majesty's Theatre in the Haymarket I was as excited as any school-girl. As a Scot, I knew just how I had to be dressed so it wasn't difficult to know the right clothes to hire—tartan skirt, brogue shoes, tam-o'-shanter hat and so on.

I was the only one to dress for the part and the only one to sing numbers from the show. When I walked on the stage of that vast, empty theatre, I could feel a rustle of excite-ment pass through the handful of theatre executives who had come to hear the auditions.

The pianist played the introduction and the other girls, who had already been heard, sat in the stalls looking up at me. I took a deep breath and sang the first number, *The Love of My Life*. The song ends with the words ...

'I'm still looking to be a wife and find the real love of my life.'

When I had finished there was complete silence. Then a little man stood up in the stalls, his face one big smile.

'Miss Gordon,' he called out, 'are you married? If not, will you marry me so you will always be there to sing my songs the way you've just sung that one?'

I brushed away the tears. For I knew at once who it must be—Frederick Loewe, the distinguished American com-poser who had written the musical score.

But there was still one more song to sing, *My Mother's Wedding Day*. When I had finished this time, there was a round of applause from the stalls and even the girls who had already auditioned joined in.

Frederick Loewe stood up again.

'She *is* Meg Brockie,' he said and he gave me the part.

So you see, two make-believe Megs have brought me good fortune—one on the stage and one on television.

That same year, in 1947, we performed an excerpt from *Brigadoon* in the Royal Variety Show before King George VI and Queen Elizabeth, now the Queen Mother.

However, people weren't quite so tolerant or broad-minded in those days and when it came to my singing *My Mother's Wedding Day* it was decided that the song was just a little too saucy to be sung before Royalty. For the whole point of the lyric was that my mother had been something of a village floozy, just as I was ...

To make this clear, the ending went something like this ...

'It was a sight beyond compare ... I ought to know for I was there ...

'There was never a day as rare ... as my Mother's Wedding Day.'

But when it came to my singing this in the Royal Variety Show it was decided to change things a little. Ted Ray, who was also on the bill, suggested we dropped the line 'I ought to know for I was there' and in its stead he came up with this alternative—'The sky was blue and the weather fair.' And that's what I sang.

On my opening night as that other Meg in *Brigadoon*, followed by my appearance before Royalty, there was no prouder mother in the world than Jockey. She had every right to be; not just because of my success but her own, too.

For it was she who had made it all possible.

Today, Mother is in her seventies. She's a bit touchy about her exact age, otherwise I would tell you!

She never misses watching a *Crossroads* episode and she is, as you can imagine, my sternest critic. But few people know that the first person to be seen on the opening programme of *Crossroads* was my own mother.

Reg Watson was all set to tape the first edition when he suddenly realized he had forgotten to book an extra—someone to walk into the motel with the camera following through the swing doors to give the impression that the viewers were also entering the motel for the first time.

As this was our first programme, naturally Mother was on hand to watch it all come to life.

Reg went up to her and explained what was wanted.

'All you have to do is to walk through the doors as though you were entering a real hotel,' he told her. 'We will be behind you with a camera.'

And that's just what happened. The studio manager tapped her on the legs with a long stick, out of camera vision, and Mother walked into the hotel as though she had just arrived to register.

No one guessed that the grey-haired, smartly dressed first arrival at Meg Richardson's newly opened hotel was the mother of the leading lady!

Whenever I am on television or making public appearances Mother is usually with me. She can remember far more of what has gone on in *Crossroads* over the years than I can.

But having a daughter on television does have its complications.

I was being interviewed by *TV Times* and Ken Roche, the feature writer who came to see me at ATV's Birmingham studios, happened to notice a stamp tray which Mother had made for me.

This is one of Mother's hobbies—she gets hold of trays and covers them with foreign stamps, sticking them on with a special liquid which hardens the surface. I don't know what it is and she has never told me—just one of her little secrets. The trays look very attractive and we sell them for charity. We've even used one in *Crossroads*.

Ken Roche asked if the *TV Times* could take a picture of Mother with one of her trays. This duly appeared. The next thing I knew was a frantic phone call from ATV's post-room saying they had two large mail bags full of used postage stamps and—please—could we do something about it? More were flooding in by every post.

Crossroads fans had read about Mother's hobby and

decided to help her by sending in all their used foreign stamps.

As more came in there was only one thing to do—we put out a special appeal on our Midlands News Bulletin, thanking everyone for sending in their stamps but asking them not to send any more.

'Mrs Gordon has plenty now,' said the news-reader. 'Thank you all very much for sending them in. But please, no more.'

Obviously, Mother had far more stamps than she could possibly handle so she took what she wanted and we sent the rest to Biddy Baxter who edits the BBC's *Blue Peter* programme. They organize an appeal every year for foreign stamps and these are then auctioned to raise money for charity. I was glad that *Crossroads* was able to join in such a good cause.

My mother is a very determined woman—with very fixed ideas. She doesn't always approve of Meg's behaviour— particularly in her choice of men-folk.

'Meg's as silly as you are' is one of her favourite sayings. But there's one thing about Meg she does approve— her non-smoking.

'If Meg doesn't have to smoke, why do you?' is another of her frequent observations.

Crossroads passed its 2,000th performance early last year and is now all set for its 2,500th early in 1975. It's just as well I was used to long runs on the stage before coming to television, the longest being just under 1,000 performances as that other Meg in *Brigadoon*.

There is, however, a big difference between being a stage actress and a television actress in a long-running serial.

When you are in the same production every night, you arrive at the theatre knowing what is expected of you and what you have to do when you get on the stage behind the footlights and face the audience.

You can vary a gesture, turn differently or move in a slightly different manner. But that's all. Everything has to be the same—every night. The words have to be the same—

66

otherwise the rest of the cast wouldn't recognize their cues.

This same routine, night after night, can be very boring for a performer and this is why most top stars fight shy of a 'run of the show' stage contract. They don't want to be tied down too long—just the first six months or so.

Think how long *The Mousetrap* has been running on the London stage and imagine what it would be like to have appeared in every performance since it was first produced twenty-two years ago. No wonder there have been so many changes in the cast over the years.

Crossroads is very different. Each episode is different; fresh lines have to be learned, fresh emotions have to be registered. Every performance is like a first night. This keeps you alert and on your toes. You just don't get *time* to be bored. New characters are brought in, new plot situations are developed.

Throughout these many changes we all work as a team and everyone gets paid the same. There are no star salaries because there are no stars.

We are often compared with *Coronation Street* but really the two serials are very different.

Coronation Street costs around £3,000 an episode and is seen twice a week.

Crossroads, originally five episodes a week and now four, is a low budget programme. Costs have increased but originally they were around £700 an episode. The pay structure is very different too.

The stars of *Coronation Street* get as much as £400 for a week's work, but as we have no star system our rates are much lower.

A special deal has been done with Equity, the actors trade union, which provides for *Crossroads* performers to be paid a flat rate for every episode in which they appear.

This works out at £40 a show—now that it is fully networked—plus normal payments for rehearsals, travelling, and subsistence allowances.

They have a similar system at the National Theatre and The Royal Shakespeare Company. Neither pay star salaries.

If a performer is lucky enough to appear in all four weekly episodes then he would be getting £160 a week but in terms of television payments this is very small, particularly as few of the cast appear in all four programmes for very long.

Fees are much lower than you would get in a normal TV play, but against this, a normal TV production is only a three weeks' engagement. In other words, three weeks' work and you are looking for another job again.

In my own case, as I mentioned earlier, I am on the staff of ATV so this means I draw my salary whether I am appearing on the screen or not.

But this is exceptional. As far as I know I am the only actress to be in this position. The arrangement goes back to my first joining the company before we went on the air, back in the fifties, and I have worked for ATV ever since.

Although *Crossroads* fees cannot be compared with TV payments for plays, we are certainly better treated than we were a few years ago. It was basically the whole question of payment and conditions of work that made me decide to quit the role of Meg Richardson.

When I walked out of *Crossroads* I made headline news. Many people thought it was just a publicity stunt but I assure you, it wasn't. I really did resign and as far as I was concerned, Meg Richardson was finished—she and I were through.

I had then been with the serial for more than three years. We were all working very hard and it seemed to me that I was working hardest of all.

So when my contract came up for renewal, I explained to the powers-that-be that the only time I had been away from the studios was at week-ends and my fee for appearing on each *Crossroads* programme was then just £30 a show.

This compared very unfavourably with other TV series and productions, even within ATV's own studios. At that time, the cast of *Emergency–Ward 10* were receiving between £150 and £200 weekly and as they only appeared twice a week, this in itself, gave them much more freedom and much less to do than working on our four programmes.

My salary as a staff member of ATV was hinged to my *Crossroads* work so, as a member of the executive staff, I still considered I wasn't being treated very fairly. The only advantage I was getting was holidays with pay—*Crossroads* pay.

The new contract I had been offered was no different to the last and as I hadn't had an increase in salary for seven years, I decided that if I was going to quit, this was the moment. I hadn't an agent. I had no man behind me. There was no one to consult. So I just went into action as Meg might have done ... on my own.

I formally sent off letters to Sir Lew Grade, Leonard Mathews, our Midlands Controller, and Reg Watson, our producer, telling them that if they didn't change the contract I would resign.

Somehow or other the *Sunday Telegraph* got hold of the news and put it on their front page. Other papers followed them. This caused the biggest rumpus *Crossroads* has ever known. The phones never stopped; ATV's switchboard was jammed.

Shoals of letter kept arriving at our Midlands studios pleading with me to stay. Others wrote to the company protesting against their treatment of poor Meg.

More papers printed more articles. The Birmingham Press was flooded with protests. TV journalists not only reported that I was leaving but they also began hazarding just how Meg's departure would be explained away on the programme. Most of them favoured sudden death in a plane crash, and this brought an even greater outcry from viewers.

The thought of Meg being deliberately killed was just too awful for them to contemplate and the mere suggestion of such a fate resulted in even more letters and phone calls of protest.

'Don't let Meg die,' wrote one woman. 'If you do I'll kill myself.'

Another woman rang me up and asked me to head a mass rally of *Crossroads* supporters. They wanted to storm the ATV studios. 'Save Meg' letters arrived in the offices of the National Press and factories in the Midlands sent us round robin letters with hundreds of signatures.

It was all very loyal and touching and I began to feel beastly and started to hate myself. If it meant so much to so many people then, surely, I thought, I owed it to them to carry on.

On the other hand, I had resigned from ATV and it was too late to do anything about it.

It was all too much for me to cope with so I decided to get away from it all and go off to Tunisia on holiday with Mother. As far as I was concerned I'd finished with Meg Richardson and I would be looking for a new job on my return.

But before I went, the BBC were soon after me with offers of work and there was also some lucrative approaches from other ITV companies, as well as advertising agencies wanting me to appear in commercials. Even while I was in Tunisia I had two cables with other ITV offers. I was also asked to tour in a play, followed by a season in Blackpool. It was very tempting to accept and return to the stage after spending so many years in television.

Meanwhile during my absence from England, Reg Watson was announcing that Meg would be making her 'last appearance about the second week of August'. This was in 1968 and he confirmed he was already at work with his writers trying to develop a dramatic departure for me.

Once again there was uproar among Meg's horrified supporters. If anyone at ATV wanted any proof of the popularity of *Crossroads* and the loyalty of our viewers, then they had it now. It was the first mass demonstration of this kind that any TV character had ever caused in Britain.

I was quite shattered—and also flattered—when friends phoned to me in Tunisia to tell me what a furore I had caused.

By the time I came back from holiday—still expecting to be leaving the programme—ATV had decided that maybe Meg ought to stay with *Crossroads* after all. We had a round table discussion and the whole business was settled amicably.

I was given my increase in salary and my appearances were cut to a maximum of three programmes a week, so this gave me my day off. I went home to tell Mother, hugged her, and we celebrated with a glass of champagne.

Naturally I was delighted with the outcome. It would have been a great wrench to have parted from Meg after such a long and happy life with her. At the same time, what really decided me to stay was the spontaneous support I was given by so many thousands of *Crossroads* fans.

I felt that if I really had walked out on Meg I would be letting them down and this is the real reason why I stayed. I'm sure I was right.

But Reg Watson had by now written me out of the series by sending Meg off to Canada to visit Sandy. Viewers saw her arrive at the airport but when the final round up of passengers was announced Meg was seen on her own—she never caught the plane.

Later, in another episode, Sandy was on the phone to Jill saying that his mother hadn't arrived in Canada and viewers were left with a mystery—what had happened to Meg?

I was out of *Crossroads* for six weeks and when the time came for me to return, the explanation given for my absence was a romantic one.

Meg, instead of going to visit Sandy in Canada, had caught a plane to Paris where she had enjoyed a brief encounter with Hugh Mortimer.

If I hadn't agreed to return to *Crossroads* then Reg would have to explain Meg's disappearance in some other way—and permanently too.

Meg would have been allowed to die—with no hope of ever returning.

Seven years have passed since all this happened and I have never regretted my decision to stay, even though remaining with the programme has cost me a great deal of money. There is no doubt that I could double, or even treble, my income if I was allowed to accept some of the very tempting offers that keep coming my way to appear on television in a commercial.

Top stars earn more than £1,000 for these appearances but I am banned and I must accept it. Under the rules of the Independent Broadcasting Authority I cannot appear in any commercial because they consider I am too well known in the role of Meg Richardson and it would appear that Meg was supporting margarine, bread, or some other household item—not Noele Gordon.

The IBA take the view that this would amount to Meg sponsoring a product and under the Television Act no such sponsorship is allowed.

It's true that a number of ITV performers such as Benny Hill and William Franklyn do appear in commercials, but they appear as themselves, not in their TV characters.

In my case, the Authority considers that just to see me on the screen, without a word being said, would be enough to identify me as Meg Richardson and I suppose they're right.

But the odd thing about all this is that BBC performers are allowed to appear in commercials in their BBC roles, which is why Dick Emery pops up as Mandy in those supermarket adverts.

Mandy may—but Meg may not!

CHAPTER FIVE

One of my most dramatic moments in *Crossroads* was the day when I was supposed to get that letter from Hugh Mortimer to say that while he was in Australia he had married someone else.

As he returned from Australia a widower—and Meg is the forgiving sort—she got re-engaged to him, but I'm quite sure if I had been treated that way in real life I wouldn't have given him a second chance even though Hugh Mortimer, played by John Bentley, has great charm and no one could be more pleased than I to have him back in the series.

When Hugh ended Meg's *first* engagement I knew what was expected of me when it came to recording the scene in which I was to receive Hugh's letter. There is nothing like a tear or two when it comes to registering sadness and disappointment but, in fact, this was the first time that Meg had ever actually been asked to cry on the screen. Till then, it had all been very much a question of the stiff upper lip, setting a good example with complete control of her own personal feelings in moments of stress and crisis.

But love is a different thing and to be jilted in love calls for only one reaction from a woman—tears.

I hadn't really discussed the scene with anyone beforehand and I don't think anyone in the studio was actually prepared for what happened in front of the cameras. At rehearsals and during the studio run-through I had been quite calm and collected but, for the real thing, I managed to rise to the occasion: real tears poured down my cheeks and it looked as if it really was the saddest moment in Meg's life. In fact it was so impressive that the studio technicians applauded me when I had finished.

Not that I remember much of their applause. By this time I was in my dressing-room—sobbing my heart out. I went on and on. I just couldn't stop.

Now I will tell you the reason why I was able to act this scene with such intense realism. When Meg Richardson broke down and cried on learning she had been jilted there was no need for me to put myself in her place—I was just myself. In other words, I relived the moment when I, too, had been jilted in real life. It's a story I have never told before but when you have heard it, you will understand why I have never married.

Only Mother and a few intimate friends know any of this but since there is such a close association with what happened to Meg and what happened to me in reality, I feel the time has come to tell you the story.

I was just a young girl—eighteen—and touring in the musical show *Black Velvet*. Our principal comedian was Ted Ray and one of our principal singers was Jean Morton, who has also had her own series for ATV in the Midlands.

While I was on tour I fell madly in love with a young Army officer—I'll call him Clive, though this wasn't his real name. He was twenty-five and we met at a party. He made a great fuss of me and as the show was visiting various provincial towns he kept coming to see me whenever he could.

During the time we were playing Liverpool and I was staying at the Adelphi Hotel, there was an air raid one night after the show and Clive came with me and the other hotel guests and staff into the cellars which had been turned into air raid shelters. As we crouched there in semi-darkness he held my hand—more to calm my fears, I thought, than to be romantic. But love can hit you at any time and at any place—even in a Liverpool cellar.

Before I realized what was happening this young Army captain, boyish and handsome in his khaki uniform, was telling me how much he loved me.

'Please, Noele,' he said, 'forget about the war—forget about the bombs ... Marry me.'

At first I thought he had just been carried away by the romanticism of the moment but when I looked at his face I knew he was quite serious. From a long way off I heard a voice saying 'If you really want me—then of course I will.' He kissed me and it was only then that I realized that I had actually accepted him.

Our existing tour had a few weeks left to run and I was under contract to continue with a further tour later in the year. I went to George Black, who was presenting the show, and told him what had happened.

'We finish in Burnley,' I told him, 'and I'm finishing too.'

'What do you mean—you're finishing too?'

'Just that—I'm leaving the stage. I'm marrying Clive. I'm giving it all up.'

George Black roared with laughter.

'You bloody little idiot,' he said, 'I'll give you three months and you'll be back."

But I was serious. The tour closed in Burnley, Ted Ray and all the others wished me luck, and I left the stage door that night to catch a train to London, determined never to be an actress again.

Clive was then stationed at Nottingham so we took a furnished house there and planned our wedding. I lived in the house with Mother while Clive was in barracks. Everything was happening just as I hoped it would; I went to Scotland to meet his parents, he bought me a beautiful engagement ring, and we were all set for a June wedding.

Before joining the Army, Clive had been studying to become a solicitor. He came from a family of lawyers and there was no doubt he had a great legal career ahead of him as soon as the war finished.

We made all sorts of plans. We were young and very much in love. It was to be a registry office wedding at Nottingham with one of Clive's fellow officers as best man and Mother had helped me choose my wedding outfit—a pale blue two-piece with cream fox fur trimmings. I can see the suit as though it was yesterday, together with matching hat, cream shoes, and gloves and bag to match as well.

As it was wartime we planned a quiet wedding; just a few close friends and my Mother, together with Clive's parents and a few army friends. Everything was set. The invitations had gone out. The honeymoon fixed.

But then, just a few days before the wedding, I had a letter from Clive breaking the whole thing off. He didn't give any real reason except that he just couldn't go through with it.

I never saw him again.

Of course I cried. I cried a lot.

Months later, mutual friends told me why Clive had made this decision. His family had put pressures on him not to marry me. They had nothing against me personally but they didn't want him to marry an actress; anyone connected with the stage would not be accepted into their family and that was that.

Eventually Mother said to me, 'What are you going to do, Noele?'

'There's only one thing I can do,' I told her, 'go back to work.'

So I caught a train to London and went straight to George Black.

'You were right,' I said, 'it didn't work. I'm back.'

'Hell,' said George, 'I only wish I'd taken a bet.'

As he had just started another tour of *Black Velvet* he put me back in the show ...

Well there it is. The only proposal I ever really took seriously—and now you all know what happened. So you see, I had only to turn back the clock and think of my own broken romance, when I had been jilted in real life, to break down sobbing for Meg Richardson when she found herself in a similar situation.

The strange part of all this is that none of the script-writers nor the production team could possibly have known of my broken romance and it was pure coincidence that such a sequence should be written into *Crossroads* for Meg Richardson. Even the arrival of the letter was the same. I had to open Meg's letter just as I had opened mine in Nottingham all those years before.

And another strange coincidence, Hugh Mortimer married an Australian. I learned later that my real life fiancé, Clive, had married an Australian girl, too.

So really, it wasn't very hard for Meg to cry!

Meg has had one other romance since then and this was also something of a disaster when it turned out that Malcolm Ryder, played by David Davenport, to whom she was married for a while, turned out to be a complete rotter and even tried to murder her by poisoning.

Ryder was supposed to be on the board of some company and he got into debt. Meg had to find £10,000 to cover up for him but unknown to Meg, he got her insurance and tried to poison her.

Actually, we never gave the name of the poison he used and none of us in the cast was ever told. While seeking a method by which they could have me slowly poisoned, the scriptwriters and researchers came across an ingredient which is in everyday use and is quite undetectable in the body. It is a certain killer and it cannot be traced by an autopsy or post-mortem.

When our producer Reg Watson heard what they had discovered he checked with our medical adviser and obtained confirmation of what they had told him. At once, all mention of the actual poison was deleted from the script and to this day I have no idea what it is.

Meg has been unlucky in love—just as I have. When Clive broke off my real-life engagement just seven days before we were to be wed, I made a vow to myself that I would never marry or give up the stage unless I met a real superman.

So this is how it's been ever since. I've worked hard at my career just as Meg has worked hard running her motel and catering business.

I suppose both of us would marry again if the right

person came along. But he hasn't yet turned up for me and he hasn't turned up for Meg, either. Like Meg, I seem to have a weakness for falling for the wrong type of man. Of course I have had *some* romances—like any other woman of my age—and I hope to have more, but I've always enjoyed my independence and most of the men I have met always want to change me. They always seem to want to mould me into the type of woman *they* want me to be, but you can't change people—they are what they are.

Don't think I'm not in favour of marriage and motherhood. I would have liked both and this is why I have enjoyed watching Roger Tonge and Jane Rossington grow up as my make-believe children.

They now call me Mother on and off the set. Between ourselves, I get a little kick out of it and no one is more delighted than I am when they come to me with their real-life problems just as though I was their real mother.

All this, of course, is no substitute for the real thing— but it's something.

There is another way in which I really *am* like Meg, or perhaps I've made Meg like me—I don't really know—but, just as Meg is opposed to couples living together, having illegitimate children, and flaunting all this in public, so I am against it too.

This seems to me to be sheer disaster from a woman's point of view.

Sooner or later the man walks out and the woman and whatever children they have are left to look after themselves —often with no income.

In my experience, ninety per cent of women need a man to look after them, anyway, and I'm sure Meg agrees with me. Marriage has always offered protection for women and though I know Women's Lib will hate me for saying this, nevertheless I believe it to be true.

Marriage, as I see it, has been devised for women's protection and the more young girls realize this the better it would be for them. Security can often bring happiness, you know.

As career women, Meg and I, we can take care of ourselves. We have our own security, are both middle-aged, and we enjoy our freedom. But this life of ours isn't for twenty-year-old girls who go around having babies without husbands. Who is going to look after them when they're forty?

It's up to every woman to work out her own attitude to life and how she wants to live. Lots of women want to be dominated by a man for this is woman's traditional role. But as Meg and I have shown, it isn't always necessary. This is why, although I always try to portray Meg as a sensible, level-headed, practical soul, I also try to make her a warm-hearted woman who needs to love and be loved. Like any woman.

I have turned down four proposals since in my life and I don't regret the decisions. When I was studying TV in New York there was a New York stockbroker who fell madly in love with me—or so he said—after meeting me at a cocktail party. He wanted me to marry him and live on Long Island. This would have meant giving up my career. I wouldn't have minded that but the trouble was that he wanted to turn me into someone else—he wasn't prepared to accept me as I am ... So I turned him down.

There was also a Hollywood agent—a very big name so perhaps I'd better not reveal it. He used to phone me every night from California when I was living in London—it must have cost him thousands of dollars in phone calls. Every call was a proposal. But I never said Yes. I just didn't love him.

Meg hasn't had any transatlantic phone calls offering her marriage yet, but I'm sure she would cope with them just as I did!

Of course we both have men friends. In fact I'm involved with a very charming man at the moment. He's eligible, too —but I don't think I'll marry him. Not that he's asked me— yet!

Although Meg has found time for a couple of romances, love doesn't work out very well for me. Love—and I mean the real thing, deep and lasting—has to be cared for; nurtured like a precious flower. If you don't work at being in love it just curls up and dies like a faded flower. But love still remains the most important ingredient in a woman's life. If it isn't then it should be.

Love-making too, is wonderful—I wouldn't have you think that I regard it as otherwise—but only if you are both in love, honestly and truly.

I am well aware that most men are terrified of self-sufficient women like Meg and me; I think perhaps this is why there have only been a couple of romances in Meg's life. But both of us would rather be in a man's company than alone. There can, however, be snags.

When I get taken out to lunch or dinner by a man, for instance, the waiters usually recognize me and ensure that I get the best table and the best attention. Most men don't like this—why should they? They resent arriving at a restaurant and taking a back seat while Meg Richardson takes over. So my menfriends just have to accept Meg as well—where I go, she goes. Me and my shadow, as it were. I just try to make a joke of it by pointing out that they're getting two girlfriends for the price of one!

Married men? Well, that isn't quite my line. I've had a few proposals of marriage from them too—like most women. But I would never break up a happy marriage—I would rather be on my own.

There *was* a man once with whom I was very much in love. I would have done anything for him but he, too, went off and married someone else.

So you see, Meg isn't the only one to suffer.

All the same, there was a time, in 1973, when many people thought I was getting married in real life—to Larry Grayson.

My engagement to Larry started as a joke but it got into the papers and so many people took it for real we didn't like to spoil things for them by telling the truth—at least not until now.

It all began when some of the *Crossroads* cast, including Ann George (Amy Turtle) and Maggie French, our production manager, went to his opening night in cabaret at the Cresta Club, Solihull.

Larry didn't know they were in the audience but for some weeks he had been making jokes about Meg Richardson, Amy Turtle, and other *Crossroads* characters in his cabaret act and in Saturday Night Variety on ITV. However, unlike some other performers, Larry always took care not to knock us or make jokes at our expense. In other words they were *friendly* jokes and since many *Crossroads* fans were in his audience he always got a good *friendly* reaction.

On this particular night he was in tremendous form and finished with an ovation. Afterwards the *Crossroads* party went backstage to see him and, as you can imagine, he was somewhat shaken to learn they had been in the audience. But when he realized they had enjoyed his gags he was soon chatting away about all the events that were currently taking place at the motel.

'How do you know all this?' asked Maggie French. 'You must be a *Crossroads* fan.'

'Indeed I am,' said Larry. 'I never miss it. Why don't you have me on the programme?'

Margaret French said nothing at the time but in the morning she told Reg Watson what had happened.

'Great,' said Reg, 'ask him on the show for Thursday.'

Maggie phoned Larry at the club that night and asked if he was serious about appearing.

'Of course,' he told her, 'I'd love to.'

So that's how it happened that he walked up to Meg Richardson at the end of one episode, completely unannounced, to complain about the room she had given him.

There was no script. Larry just made it all up as he went along. I enjoyed it just as much as the viewers and, like them, I had no idea what he would say next.

He pretended he had been camping down the road and had booked in the night before because of the bad weather. Then he started to complain—at just about everything. His aches and pains were worse than ever!

He'd fallen over Amy Turtle's bucket (who would leave a bucket underneath the bed, of all places?); the whole chalet was dripping with water ('there's a couple of fish in the bath') and on top of all this, there had been something gnawing away at the woodwork all night ('they must be your ferrets').

At the mention of the word 'ferrets' I collapsed, helpless. The programme had to be faded out ... Meg Richardson was speechless, doubled up with laughter.

It so happened that I had just received a letter from a male *Crossroads* fan who had offered to take me out. He wrote 'I think you are a beautiful angel and I would like to walk out with you and take you to the pictures. But you might prefer to play with my ferrets which I keep at the bottom of the garden. They are sweet little creatures and don't answer back like the wife ...'

I had written back and told him I thought it would be unfair for me to come between him and his ferrets.

Reg and some of the others knew about the letter and must have mentioned it to Larry so you will understand why, when he came out with his final joke about my ferrets being in his woodwork, I just fell apart.

'Oh, you wicked man,' I said to him as soon as I could speak again and back I fell, once more, into a chair.

We have had this kind of relationship ever since. He always makes me laugh. He is quite the funniest man I have ever met and, also, one of the kindest.

When Thames Television featured me on *This is Your Life* they secretly contacted Larry at the Wakefield Theatre Club, where he was currently appearing, and asked him to be the surprise guest at the end of the programme. He agreed at once—providing he could get back to Wakefield in time to appear at 11.30. So after his appearance on the show, Thames TV had a car waiting to whisk him to the station. He arrived at the stage door at 11.10 p.m.

It was *This is Your Life* which started talk of Larry being in love with me.

All the *Crossroads* cast were in on the secret that I was

to be featured on the show—all except me, of course. Even Mother knew, but she never told me. All that I knew was that I had a call from Reg Watson to take part in a rehearsal for a promotion trailer which was to be made at our Birmingham studios. In this particular short promotion spot I had to walk through the doors into the reception, say something about *Crossroads*, and finish up with 'this is my manager, played by Ronnie Allen'.

Ronald Allen was waiting at the counter for me and the scene went off without a hitch at rehearsals. However, when it came to the actual take, I came through the doors and started to say the wrong sentence. So I stopped, stood there, and said nothing.

It was not until later that I heard just how near I had come to ruining the whole opening of *This is Your Life*; for by this time, Eamonn Andrews had switched places with Ronnie and it was he who was waiting for me.

When the floor manager saw what had happened he signalled to Eamonn who promptly ran out of the studio while Ronnie Allen went back to where he had been sitting at rehearsals.

It would obviously have spoiled the whole surprise element if I had seen Eamonn before the actual moment of the pick-up.

Anyway, I just said I was sorry, went back through the doors, and did my entrance again. This time there was no slip-up. Eamonn was back into position so my surprise and shock was even more real than anyone could possibly realize. For just a moment before, Ronnie Allen had been sitting there and then, as if by magic, it was Eamonn. It was all very cleverly done.

It was a fantastic experience—nerve shattering too. I couldn't speak—only gasp.

Mother had packed my clothes—without telling me. One of the *This is Your Life* team came with me on the train to London to tape the rest of the programme and I wasn't even allowed to leave the compartment. When I wanted to go to the toilet they made me wear a blindfold!

83

This was to stop me seeing any of the other *Crossroads* folk because, unknown to me, they were all on the same train and I didn't see them until they came on the show later in the TV studio.

Larry Grayson followed them. I nearly fainted. I knew he was appearing in Wakefield and I just couldn't believe he had come all that way—just for a couple of minutes on TV with me. And that's when our 'romance' was born.

'Noele,' he said when he walked on, 'I do love you.'

I knew he was joking so I carried on in the same vein. 'I keep asking him to marry me but he won't,' I explained.

Larry's answer was gallant and to the point.

'I will then,' he said.

After all, what *else* could he say?

So I carried on joking ...

'Remember,' I told him, 'you've said it now. And millions of viewers have heard you too.'

Well, that started it all. We both had congratulatory telegrams, flowers, and phone calls. I had a stack of beautiful engagement cards from viewers wishing me every happiness and wherever Larry went he was asked the date of the wedding.

I suppose it was naughty of us both to joke about getting married in the first place but at the time, it all seemed innocent enough and neither of us thought so many people would take it for real.

Looking back, I don't think any real harm was done. We are still great friends—even if we aren't engaged—and when I in turn was invited to be on Larry's *This is Your Life*, I was delighted to take part.

Since then, I have made several appearances with Larry in variety shows for ATV and he also came to Birmingham while rehearsing for his pantomime at Bristol to make a second appearance in *Crossroads* for our Christmas edition.

This time he was a surprise Father Christmas.

His Bristol pantomime, by the way, in which he appeared as Wishee Washee in *Aladdin*, broke all box-office records. I went to see him and was very thrilled to see he had a picture of the two of us together on the table in his dressing-room. He takes it everywhere with him.

He still keeps cracking gags about us all. When he was in the Coventry Theatre revue we all went to see him and we thoroughly enjoyed all his jokes about us.

I hope he'll be able to come back to *Crossroads* again soon—he knows that we will all make him very welcome. Meanwhile as you may have noticed, Meg often gets phone calls from him.

But between ourselves, Meg Richardson isn't all that keen on having him back when he rings up to book a room. He caused such a furore last time and made so many complaints that Meg always tries to put him off. Up till now she's succeeded, too. For my part, I have the feeling that whenever Larry finds himself appearing in the Midlands he will manage to break down Meg's resistance and book into *Crossroads* again.

Just as I make fun of him, as Meg, in those fake TV phone calls so he, in return, keeps up the relationship by saying things about Meg Richardson. I don't mind in the least. It has now become part of his act and there's nothing spiteful or malicious in his remarks. He puts me in his act whenever he feels like it.

'I'm so ill,' he says. 'Everard told me to see my doctor. Anyway he was very reassuring. Everything's in perfect working order.'

And then he adds, 'Noele Gordon *will* be pleased.'

He waits for the laughter and says, 'She'll murder me!'

I now have to give him a regular supply of signed photographs of myself—he gets so many requests at stage doors for Meg's picture as well as his.

When he makes personal appearances—opening shops and that sort of thing—the women shoppers always want to know how Meg is and he's often jokingly warned:

'Behave yourself, Larry, or we'll tell Meg Richardson about you.'

This is the kind of relationship that has built up between

us—a fun relationship. And if it gives you all a laugh then we're happy, too.

What I would really like is to be in a TV comedy series with him one day ...

I'm sure it would be quite hilarious.

Mind you, I think being married to Larry Grayson would be hilarious, too. We'd never be short of laughs.

Stewart Knowles, a writer in *TV Times,* has said that I 'tread a fine line between the lady and the tomboy'. I suppose this is true. For I *can* fly a plane; I *can* drive a racing car; I *did* take up skin-diving for the TV series *Your Kind of Sport*; I've also been down a coal-mine; ridden an elephant and a camel; dressed up as a clown and been in a cage of lions ... all in the interest of television.

Of all this, it was the mine that impressed me the most. It was a very deep pit at Cannock Chase and a new one; for the last hundred yards we had to crawl on our hands and knees to the actual coal-face where the men were working. It's something I will never forget and that's why, earlier this year, I had the greatest sympathy for the miners. I've seen how they have to work—and where. All the money in the world could never compensate them sufficiently for what they have to endure.

I keep all this tomboy stuff away from Meg Richardson of course. She is really much more feminine than I am in real life. I know I have a very hearty laugh and it's not a theatrical one—by that I mean I don't fake it—I really do laugh loudly. But I don't think this kind of laugh is right for Meg's image and you will never hear her break into wild guffaws.

People who work with me on *Crossroads* tell me I'm a very forthright person. I suppose I am. I don't suffer fools gladly and I think Meg has far more patience than I have.

Sometimes I get compliments about my eyes which is rather nice because I, too, think they are rather special and that I'm lucky to have them, but when anyone tells me what lovely hair I have then they usually get one of my

86

loudest guffaws.

For my hair is dyed—in the interests of television again! The true colour is very dark brown, almost black, and when I first appeared on TV the make-up people found it a great problem—it looked much too dark and lifeless on the screen. So they used to blow gold dust all over me—I was always covered in the stuff—but it gave my hair highlights and improved my whole TV appearance.

But I became so fed up with the mess it made that I asked the make-up girls what would be the best colour for my hair.

'Why not go red?' they suggested.

So off I went to my old friend Raymond and came back to the studios—a red-head. And I've been a red-head ever since.

Now of course, with colour TV, my hair looks better than ever but it costs a fortune to keep it looking that way and if you knew the hours I spend at Raymond's you wouldn't envy me at all.

Although I visit the hairdressers weekly to preserve the Meg Richardson image, there is someone else working very hard behind the scenes who, more than anyone, maintains Meg's TV appearance.

She is, in fact, one of my closest friends in ATV's Studio Centre at Birmingham—someone whose face you have never seen and whose name is never on the screen credits. She is quite unknown to viewers, yet without her I would be completely lost.

Alexandra Cope has been my make-up artist for the past eight years. Alex, twenty-eight, who started her career as a dancer, answered an advertisment for make-up assistant in our early days; ATV trained her and she has been with us ever since.

Larry Grayson has nicknamed her 'Slack Alex'—after his 'Slack Alice' character that he jokes about. But Alex really isn't slack at all. She works very hard and every Thursday morning at nine-fifteen I sit in a chair in a blue smock in the Make-up Department while Alex goes to work.

It takes her an hour to get me ready. For a start, she uses a Max Factor theatrical base applied with a moist sponge and blended as lightly as possible to avoid giving me a flat, dull look.

The whole purpose of television make-up is very different to the use of cosmetics for stage appearances or everyday life. TV make-up cannot be heavy—it has to be realistic and natural but at the same time, it has to withstand the rigours of intense studio lighting which can age you enormously.

After that pancake base Alex, using a sable brush, lightens out parts of my face which could become shadowed in the studio—especially round the eyes and mouth.

She then shades in a clean jaw line with a long-handled brush—like a painter. In fact I've often sat there, watched Alex at work in the mirror, and made the comparison in my mind between making up someone for television—and painting a picture.

I once asked her about this and Alex agreed that, in fact, that is just what she always tries to do—'to paint a picture of what Meg Richardson should be like.'

Finally, Alex goes to work on my eye make-up. This is again very light—to accentuate my eyes. For this she has a blue eye liner and navy-blue mascara.

I think she does a great job and I only wish I could do as well myself when I am away from the studios.

We also experiment with different shades of lipsticks. From time to time, Alex will turn up with a new colour which she has found in a beauty salon and we try it out on the programme.

My hair goes into heated rollers for five to ten minutes and then Meg Richardson is ready to cope with *Crossroads*.

But there's something I have learned over the years—and Alex agrees with me—make-up cannot *always* enhance a woman—not even Meg Richardson.

If you *feel* good—you will *look* good. There's no doubt that, whether you're a man or a woman, your mental state will affect your physical appearance. Even a phone call from the right person at the right moment can improve your looks.

There have been many times when I have had private worries, moments of indecision, or even a bad cold and on these occasions, despite her skill with her colouring and pencilling, Alex can never succeed in making me look my best.

When these occasions arrive we both have to accept the situation and poor Meg suffers accordingly.

Alex also helps me in many other ways ... by looking after my studio laundry; doing the odd shopping in her lunch break and taking messages for me.

There are of course, many people working behind the scenes to make *Crossroads* a success, but as far as I, personally, am concerned Alex is one of those who contributes the most.

Meg Richardson wouldn't be quite the same without her —and nor would I.

CHAPTER SIX

Before taking you any further behind the scenes of *Crossroads* I will now tell you more about the man who first brought us all to life ... Brisbane-born Reg Watson.

Reg and I have worked together for eighteen years, so you can imagine how shocked and sad I was earlier last year when he told me he was leaving *Crossroads*, the show he had created, to return to his native Australia.

Reg is now working there as Head of Drama for an Australian production company. I know it was just as big a wrench for him to leave us as it has been for us to see him go.

We all miss him terribly. But we are carrying on with *Crossroads* in the same pattern and production format he laid down for us during the 2,000-odd episodes he has produced.

Crossroads is also seen in Australia, by the way, so for some years, Reg will be able to see the programmes he made here in England—all over again in Australia.

We first met at the old Television House in Kingsway when I walked into his office. I knew from his reaction that he had never heard of me but we travelled up in the train to Birmingham—during a snowstorm, I remember—together with Ned Sherrin, who was later to discover David Frost and launch him in *That Was the Week That Was* on BBC TV.

Ned, Reg, and I—together with the late Philip Dorte, ATV's first Midlands Controller—were the company's pioneers for their Midlands operation.

Ned Sherrin was responsible for news and current affairs programmes and Reg handled light entertainment.

Reg joined us with a commercial background, having worked in Australia radio since he was sixteen. He came to England twenty years ago on a three months visit at the start of commercial television and has stayed until this year—only returning to Australia on holidays.

It was he who launched me in *Lunch Box*, an entertainment-magazine styled programme on which I was the hostess. We had a resident group—the Jerry Allen Trio—resident singers who were changed from time to time; plus guest appearances by personalities visiting the Midlands. It was really a chat show combined with light entertainment.

Reg and I must have done more than 5,000 television programmes together, including *Crossroads, Lunch Box,* and other shows and they all stem from that first meeting at Television House.

I knew when he first spoke to me that we would be able to work together. We understood each other and spoke the same language. In addition, Reg has always been able to give me the confidence and encouragement every performer needs. We have a tremendous professional *rapport* and our relationship is unique in British television, for no other TV performer has worked exclusively on such a basis with any other TV producer for so long.

There has never been any romance between us but we are very close—both professionally and away from the studios. He is one of my dearest friends and when I heard he was leaving us I broke down. That night I cried myself to sleep and, although it is months since he left, I still feel lost without him.

We respected each other's judgement and many's the time I have gone to him with various suggestions, even complaints, about the way Meg Richardson was expected to behave. Sometimes he would agree and get things changed. On other occasions he would stand firm. As a producer, Reg was never averse to hearing another person's viewpoint but if he thought he was right and they were wrong he would say so.

'Nolly,' he used to say on those occasions, 'you act—and I'll produce.'

I would always accept that.

I think the main reason he gave me so much help and confidence over the years is that, unlike many other TV producers, he always had a tremendous feeling and sympathy for actors and actresses.

He understood that a performer must have an audience— all the time. This meant that when, as Meg Richardson, I had to run through my lines at rehearsal it was a tremendous comfort to know that Reg was there in the control room watching me and listening to what I was saying. This gave me an extra confidence. I knew that if I was moving badly, or putting the wrong emphasis on a situation, he would tell me.

No performer can judge his own performance. With Reg around I never had to worry and he was always there—at rehearsals and at the final take in the studio. It was part of his policy that he should be there. Not just for me but for everyone else in the cast. He wasn't content, like so many other producers, to watch the episodes in his office over closed circuit.

We all work better if we have an audience and Reg understood this. This is why he knew how to get the best out of us by letting us know he was there ... watching.

When Reg began *Crossroads* he was starting from scratch. No one in British television had ever attempted to produce a daily serial before.

His brief, however, wasn't just to produce a daily serial —he also had to devise a serial with a Midlands flavour and background.

It has been said that you can tell a Midlander by the shamrock in his turban. In a way, this is true. The Midlands combines modern architecture and old world charm. No two accents are alike. It is a mixture of many accents and many different people.

When Reg was given the original format of a Midlands motel and launched our adventures on the screen, he was criticized in some quarters for not having enough Midlanders visiting the motel.

But of course, he was right not to do so. For Midlanders do not visit Midlands motels—except for the odd meal. The guests are always visitors to the area, as with any other motel, and it would have been factually incorrect to have Midlands personalities staying at residents.

At the beginning of *Crossroads* there were, in fact, few motels in Britain and those that did exist, although respectable and well run, suffered from the stigma that they were merely places where couples went for the illicit week-end.

I am sure that *Crossroads* helped to change this image. Britain's motels are now accepted as part of the everyday scene of our travelling way of life.

Once it was decided that Reg should produce our daily serial he began auditioning performers to portray the various roles that had been created.

In the early days he wrote a sample script which, as he admitted, was 'very difficult stuff'.

Each potential character was given this script which involved, in the case of male actors, a young man looking back on his childhood. Girls had to act a situation facing them upon entering a convent.

Every applicant was given this sample script and told to learn it within two hours. When the time period had elapsed they had to return to the studio and perform the material they had learned before the television camera, while Reg watched in the control room. Quite a nerve-racking experience—especially as none of them had been inside a TV studio before.

Reg however, was looking for certain qualities and he knew this was the best way to find them. He sought sincerity, courage, and the ability to cope with the unexpected.

At one of these tests, in our early days, he was auditioning Beryl Johnstone, from the Alexandra Repertory Company, for the part of my sister, Kitty Jarvis. Reg placed her in front of the cameras and she at once said, 'Would you mind shooting from the other side—this isn't my best angle.'

Reg told her, 'If you get this job, dear, you'll forget all about angles. We'll shoot you from every angle imaginable.'

Beryl, as you know, was one of the original *Crossroads* stalwarts and I have told you how we dealt in our story line with her tragic death.

For Reg however, it also meant he was faced with a great practical problem in the studio on the day she died.

Beryl had not been well for some while. She lived nearby at Cheltenham and on the morning she was due to come to the studios to tape the first programme of the week, Reg had a phone call to say that Beryl had died in the night.

It so happened that this was a week in which Beryl was completely involved in the plot. In fact, she was appearing in twenty-six separate scenes, in a situation that had Joy Andrews (Mrs Hope) going through Customs, on her return from Corsica, with an antique clock which had been used by crooks—unknown to her—as a hiding place in which to smuggle some jewels.

Reg had to come to the studio and tell us all what had happened. We were stunned It was our first *Crossroads* death and as far as I was concerned, I took it very badly. I am an only child and Beryl and I were very close. I had begun to regard her as the first close relative I had ever had, apart from my parents. When she died it was like losing my own sister.

Reg took it all very calmly—at first. Straightaway he had to reorganize the scripts. Every scene in which Beryl was due to appear had to be rewritten. There was no question of not going ahead with the story and Beryl's involvement. The pattern of the daily serial and the stories it tells cannot be changed overnight, otherwise every situation, for weeks to come, would be thrown out of alignment—to the puzzlement of viewers.

Sitting down at his typewriter in the production office Reg produced whole new scenes for us. We had to learn the new dialogue on the spot—and forget what we had learned earlier in the week.

Joy Andrews had the most difficult task as she was the

one to be most involved in the situation. Reg had to rewrite her scenes with Beryl so that Joy, as Mrs Hope, one of the motel directors, was able to tell the story on her own. It was cleverly done and no one spotted any difference, but as far as Joy was concerned it seemed to her that she was asking herself questions to which she already knew the answers! Very complicated.

However, we all managed to cope. Then at the end of the week, there came the saddest moment of all when we went to Cheltenham to attend the funeral.

Till then, Reg had thrown himself into the studio crisis with such vigour and determination there had been no time for personal grief. It wasn't until the funeral that the realisation Beryl had gone really hit him.

This is the kind of personal involvement that arises when you are part of a community that has been built around you over the years. As performers we are all a very close-knit unit. We may be living our fake lives at *Crossroads* every week, but now and then reality steps in.

There was a similar situation with the death of Jack Hayes, an old-time music hall comic. Jack had been appearing for us as an extra but he did so well that his part was enlarged and we got to the point where he was just about to plan a wedding with Ann George, who has been one of our *Crossroads* fixtures since our early days.

Plans for the wedding had to be cancelled and the whole sequence scrapped.

When this kind of thing happens it is the producer's responsibility to deal with the situation and ensure that *Crossroads* continues.

Over the years there have been many backstage dramas. Reg coped with them all and I'm sure his successor, Jack Barton, will be able to do the same.

One of these unexpected situations which Reg had to handle and which involved me personally took place when Meg was jilted on the eve of her wedding to Hugh Mortimer (John Bentley).

Meg was supposed to hear the news while on holiday in

Tunisia and her son, Sandy, was to arrive there with her wedding clothes only to be told that the wedding would not in fact be taking place.

This mother-and-son situation was obviously an integral part of the story so you can imagine Reg's consternation when he had a phone call to say that Roger Tonge had been in an accident with his Mini near his home at Harborne, Birmingham.

Another car had pulled out in front of him, Roger had been flung through the windscreen, and badly cut by sharp glass splinters on his face.

His right eyelid was severed, his cheeks and forehead slashed. His face had needed no less than eighty stitches!

The crash happened a week before Roger was due in the studio and he phoned Reg to tell him he just couldn't appear. Reg went to see him in hospital and he found Roger looking terrible. His forehead, scarred and bruised, protruded about seven inches and he had two beautiful black eyes.

Reg was equal to the occasion.

'What do you mean you can't make it?' he asked. 'You're looking fine.'

In vain, Roger protested.

'You're going to be in that studio on Wednesday for your scene with Meg whether you like it or not,' was Reg's retort.

Roger's parents, and the doctors too, realized that Reg's firmness was, in part, intentional and necessary if he was to get Roger working again as soon as possible.

Reg came back to us all, told us how disfigured Roger was looking but warned us to carry on as usual when he arrived and not to react or make any mention of his facial injuries.

But when Roger turned up in a wheel-chair I just couldn't believe my eyes. He looked so awful that I went to Reg in the control room and told him we would have to scrap the scene.

'I can't appear with him looking like that,' I told him.

'He looks worse than Frankenstein's monster. We're not making horror films you know. You'll terrify every viewer in the country.'

'Nonsense, Nolly,' said Reg, 'he looks great—perfect.'

I decided Reg Watson had gone slightly mad. I simply couldn't believe he was serious. It seemed to me that the strain of producing *Crossroads* had finally caught up with him and he was heading for a nervous breakdown.

'Reg,' I said, 'you can't do it.'

'Oh yes I can,' he said, and showed me the extra lines of dialogue he had written to cover Roger's injuries.

'All you have to do is to ask him what he's done to his face and he'll tell you he walked into a plate glass window at Cairo airport on the way over. Now forget all about it. It'll work out fine.'

Reg fixed up Roger with dark glasses to hide his black eyes and the glasses were explained away by playing the scene on a sun-drenched patio at the Tunisian hotel where I was supposed to be staying.

Roger of course, had no time to learn his lines so he sat in a chair picking up a newspaper and a book and occasionally glancing at them.

On an inside page, Reg had pasted his lines so all that Roger had to do was to read them. Because of his dark glasses no one spotted this and we both carried on as though nothing was wrong.

This real-life incident of Roger's crash and his arrival at the studios in a wheel-chair made such an impact on Reg that, some years later, he used the identical situation on the screen.

Sandy was to be taken to hospital, following a fake *Crossroads* crash, spend weeks there in a coma, and then return to us in a wheel-chair.

When it happened to Roger in real life, we kept it all a secret. But when it was to happen to Roger in his role of my son, we let 14,000,000 viewers join in.

Incidentally, although Reg had warned all the cast and studio technicians not to bat an eyelid when Roger first turned up in his wheel-chair with his battered face, there was one person he forgot to prepare for the shock.

This was the nurse in our First Aid section. She was going to have the job of dressing his wounds and putting fresh bandages on his face.

But when Roger wheeled himself into her surgery she was totally unprepared for what she saw.

The nurse fainted.

Reg Watson's departure has affected us all in different ways. Jane Rossington, who plays my daughter, went along with Roger to tape a little farewell message. This was the idea of one of our scriptwriters, Ian Scrivens. He had arranged for us all to record an individual message and the tape was given to Reg when he left for Australia.

Roger and Jane taped their messages together. Roger said some words and Jane followed him. At the end of her message Roger noticed that Jane's eyelashes were falling off —tears were pouring down her cheeks.

'Oh, Roger,' she sobbed. 'It wasn't until I said "good-bye" that I realized Reg was really going. He *will* come back to us, won't he?'

Roger didn't know what to say. To them, for the past ten years, Reg has been like an uncle. They have grown up under his professional guidance. Their acting lives have been built around him, just as mine has.

The three of us—as regular performers—are all that remains of the original *Crossroads* cast who met in that bare rehearsal room just ten years ago.

Losing Reg has been so totally unexpected we are still not used to the idea of not having him around. In the years that he has produced our serial many performers have come and gone and come back again, so it's only to be expected that we should feel Reg Watson will return to us one day.

As to whether he really will ... I just don't know.

Meanwhile, he has been replaced by another old friend of mine—Jack Barton.

Jack also used to direct me during my *Lunch Box* days

and it was during this period that he met the Duke of Bedford who made a guest appearance on the programme.

They got on well together and when the Duke offered him an executive post at Woburn Abbey, Jack left us to join his organization.

But after four years, Jack decided he would like to return to the hurly-burly of television and he has now been directing *Crossroads* for the past five years.

He has spent all his working life in show business, after running away from school to join a circus. He has worked in the theatre as an actor, singer, and dancer and has produced all types of shows, from Shakespeare to revue.

Now that Jack Barton is at the helm we may see several changes in the *Crossroads* cast and new situations developed. All producers are individuals and have their own ideas; it's their job to create our TV existence in the first place.

For a start, don't be surprised if Meg Richardson gets left a legacy—of a beautiful Silver Shadow Rolls-Royce.

Jack has decided to make use of the Rolls that I bought myself last year—by having me drive it sometimes in *Crossroads*. I will also be using it when I make personal appearances.

Last year I sold my house at Ross-on-Wye and it's really the money from the house that has paid for the car. I have my own number plate—NG10—which I have transferred from car to car over the years. Whenever Meg has to be at the wheel of a car they always use the car that I have in real life.

This needed no explanation when I had a Ford or a Triumph but now that it's a Rolls the scriptwriters will have to explain Meg's sudden acquisition.

As far as I'm concerned it's no status symbol. I've always wanted to own the best car in the world and now I've got it.

Mother was as thrilled as I when the car was delivered but now that I have it I'm not taking my Rolls out in the rain. I've opened an account with a taxi firm for the first time—just for wet days.

But with or without Meg Richardson owning a Rolls-Royce, I'm sure the essential format of *Crossroads* will remain unchanged. The programme remains as popular with viewers as when we first started and I don't think Jack Barton would want to change its over-all appeal.

New faces and new plots—yes. But not *Crossroads* itself.

CHAPTER SEVEN

As the world's longest running daily serial we hold many records and one of which we are especially proud is that we give work to 1,000 actors and actresses every year, including extras and walk-ons.

No other television programme in Britain employs so many Equity members and it has been the job of Margaret French, our production manager over the years, to find the faces and personalities to fit the various characters which our serial has created.

Maggie, as we call her, works closely with our new producer Jack Barton now that he has taken over from Reg Watson but like me, she had been associated with Reg in various ATV productions since the company first came on the air in 1956 in the Midlands, and she has worked on *Crossroads* from the start.

Maggie was brought up in show business, just as I was, and toured the music halls when she was fourteen with her sister, Eva. Their act was first known as the Margaret Sisters, a dancing duo.

Then she was with the Tiller Girls for a while and even appeared with her sister in a pantomime at the Alexandra Theatre, Birmingham—never realizing that one day she would be sitting in the stalls and booking actors and actresses from the theatre's own repertory company.

Maggie joined ATV after being with the old ABC TV company as a trainee production assistant. She worked with me on *Lunch Box* and was also working on many other Midlands programmes such as *Midland Profile*, *Paper Talk*, and a cabaret show called *Rainbow Room*.

With this kind of experience she was a natural choice as production manager of *Crossroads*.

Since the whole idea of the serial was built around my role of Meg, Maggie's main job was to first find the dozen or so regular characters who would comprise my family and my staff at the motel.

As it was to be a Midlands serial, Maggie had to find Midlands actors and actresses who could portray the various people that had been created by producer Reg Watson and his script team.

Essentially, they were looking for character faces, people in whom viewers could believe. Performers who didn't look like performers at all.

Maggie and Reg picked nearly all of them from the two local repertory companies in Birmingham itself—the Derek Salberg Company at the Alexandra and the Birmingham Repertory Company.

They went to both these companies, by arrangement with the managements, and all the actors and actresses currently appearing were assembled on the stage for Reg to explain what it was all about.

They were then invited to our old studios at Aston, a converted cinema, and asked to read an audition script. Each script, as near as possible, portrayed various aspects of the characters for which they were being auditioned and those who came the closest to our requirements were engaged.

Thirty performers were tested—ten of them given jobs.

The others gave Maggie personal details of themselves, age, height, measurements and so on, and these were placed in her files to form the nucleus of our casting department.

'We were looking for people who could keep talking,' recalls Maggie. 'None of the actors we engaged had ever been on television before. We were, in fact, assembling a TV repertory company.

'We wanted experienced actors, but we wanted people who could adapt not only to the new medium of television but also the new techniques which would be required to produce a daily TV serial on a five-days-a-week basis—as it was when we started.'

As well as first finding the regular cast and adding to them over the years, Maggie also has to find the many extras that we use. These have to be members of Equity and we always try and give as much work as we can to old pro's who are now out of the business but have just the kind of professional background we need.

For a start, we asked Equity to send round a letter to all their members in the Midlands and, from the first applicants, we picked a dozen regulars.

This number has now grown to over five hundred—all on our files in the Casting Department.

There are three rates of payment, agreed with Equity. For a small part, in which they are not required to speak or be identified, the actor gets £6 a programme.

If the performer is to be individually identified, such as a chauffeur, policeman, or someone like that, then he gets £11.

The top daily payment of £16 is for extras who are not only individually identified but also have to speak scripted lines.

Quite a few extras have done so well that they have later been engaged for more important roles. Peggy Ashby, who plays Beryl Gibson, the girlfriend of Wilf's brother Isaac, is now one of our regulars. She began as an extra.

Local drama schools also send us artists to audition. This is how we found Peter Graham who first started with us, when he was very young, as a walk-on.

Peter was especially written into the story in the character of Tony Scott, the young boy who is a friend of Sandy and confined to a wheel-chair. Audrey Noble plays his mother, who gets up at 5.45 each morning to wash and dress him as he has no movement below his armpits.

The idea for this character came after Sandy injured his spine and viewers saw him in a wheel-chair for the first time.

One viewer to contact us was Noel Crane, who lives at Ryton. Mr Crane rang up to congratulate Roger on his performance and said that he, himself, had broken his neck two years previously in a swimming accident and was now confined to a wheel-chair for the rest of his life. He added he would be happy to assist us with any further advice we might need in order to ensure Sandy's authentic performance.

As is usual under these circumstances, our researchers had already done a tremendous amount of work concerning Roger's portrayal of a paraplegic, at the Robert Jones and Agnes Hunt Orthopaedic Hospital at Oswestry.

Roger also had made several visits there to be shown how to manipulate his wheel-chair correctly and to talk things over with real life paraplegics.

However when we heard from Mr Crane we were so impressed with the story of his courage and how he is coping with life that Reg Watson decided to have a similar situation in *Crossroads*—not only as a tribute to Noel Crane but also to help others who might find themselves in similar circumstances.

This then, is exactly how the character of the wheelbound Tony Scott came to be created and Peter Graham brought back into the programme.

Peter himself has spent a lot of time with Mr Crane, who manages to lead a very full life despite his handicap. He had gadgets to open doors, write, eat, drink, and so forth. All this had been faithfully copied in our *Crossroads* character of Tony Scott.

Maggie French was born in Birmingham and she knows the area well. This helps her to pick authentic Midlands types when required, but of course as a motel we have all types and all nationalities passing through. When it comes to casting family relations she has to find facial resemblance wherever possible but for the rest of the characters she really has to visualize them as she herself sees them.

'It's like being handed a book,' she says. 'You read the story and you choose the people as you see them. I worked with Reg for so long we really did share the same wavelength. We rarely disagreed on the choice of performers.'

Television however, doesn't demand the versatility from

104

its performer in quite the same way as stage repertory companies. We are not looking for actors who can play any part from eighteen to eighty. If we want an eighteen-year-old, then we engage an eighteen-year-old. If we want someone of seventy, then it's a seventy-year-old who gets the job.

Maggie engages the exact character as she sees it— there and then, not an artist who can *become* what she wants.

Sometimes she hires someone whom she thinks will be ideal from their photograph which is on her files. But when they turn up they may have changed—grown a beard or let their hair get longer.

We had a role available for a policeman but when the actor whom Maggie had picked turned up for the part he had hair to his shoulders and was sporting a beard.

The director rang through to Maggie's office and told her what had happened.

'Put him on the phone,' she said. Maggie then told the actor that unless he shaved off his beard and had his hair cut he couldn't possibly be accepted as a Midlands police officer.

The actor agreed at once and went to the hairdressers. Within half an hour he had returned with short back and sides and minus the beard.

Maggie's filing system is very simple. Statistics such as age, height, weight, and hair colour are listed under each artist's name, together with any additional details such as specialized dialects and details of previous television appearances. A picture is stapled to each sheet of particulars. Pink paper is used for girls; blue for boys.

These two colours are for artists who have actually been seen by either Maggie or the producer.

If a performer, or their agent, has written in and they haven't yet been seen, then we use the colours yellow for males and green for females.

Our Production Office also has a somewhat unusual filing system—male actors are filed in three categories.

These are under twenty, twenty to thirty, and over fifty. The three sections relate to their real ages.

For women, we are much more gallant. They are filed under the Playing Ages, i.e. the age they look on the screen.

A discreet difference.

Everyone who appears on the programme is personally interviewed—even the extras. Some London theatrical agencies specialize in block bookings of extras, especially for films. A casting director will ring up and order 'Fifty well dressed men and women in evening clothes to appear as gamblers in a casino.' Or 'Twenty-five down and outs for a scene on the Thames embankment.' This cuts down the time taken to cast any particular scene but, at the same time, it doesn't leave the producer with the final choice as to what artist he thinks will do the best job.

In *Crossroads* there are no block bookings—everyone is seen beforehand.

Our Casting Office receives an average of twenty letters a day from agents seeking auditions for their clients or else from performers seeking work direct.

Everyone who applies gets sent a form which they then have to fill up and return, giving personal details, clothing measurements, and so forth.

But don't all rush to appear on *Crossroads*.

The last time I checked, we had a list of over 2,000 actors and actresses waiting to be auditioned.

When extras arrive for the first time to work in a TV studio, Maggie gives them a fifteen-minute lecture on what to expect; how a television programme is put together and the various Do's and Don'ts about appearing on the screen.

First, they must understand they are only being employed on the basis of casual labour. No extra can expect to make a living out of television for no director is going to use the same people over and over in different scenes. If he did, viewers would recognize them at once and the whole atmosphere of reality would be ruined.

Extras also have to understand that a TV studio has hidden microphones everywhere—behind plants, furniture, and other objects. The whole place is bugged and everything said is relayed direct to the control room.

If an extra makes any disparaging remarks about Meg Richardson looking a little the worse for wear or some such observation, then it is going to be heard straight away.

We had one extra who carried on for ten minutes, between rehearsals, about what he thought of Meg, *Crossroads*, the scripts, and everything connected with the serial. Unknown to him, he was standing near one of our hidden mikes.

The director heard every word he said. That man has never worked on the show since and, to this day, I don't suppose he knows why.

Extras must also be told to move slowly for every action in front of a camera is ten times larger than on a stage in a theatre. A quick arm movement or a sudden jerk of the head will appear completely out of proportion within the narrow confines of a small screen and look quite grotesque.

Punctuality is essential. Many of our extras are also variety acts, used to working in clubs and previously in music halls. In this branch of show business no one minds very much if a performer turns up ten minutes late for rehearsal, but in a television studio sixty people can be kept hanging around with nothing to do if a particular extra isn't on the set ready to work when the moment comes to make a start.

Discipline in television is also essential. Our floor manager—the man in charge of what goes on in front of the cameras on the studio floor—once said to an extra, 'All right, dear, you're finished.'

The woman took him at his word and went home. But all he meant to convey was that she had finished the run-through. The scene itself had yet to be taped and we hadn't even had the dress rehearsal.

Half an hour later, when the dress rehearsal was about to start, this particular guest at *Crossroads* was nowhere to be found. The director made a frantic phone call to Maggie

French who at once realised what had happened. She rang the woman's home, found she had just returned, and got her to come back immediately—by taxi.

Now Maggie tells every extra—'Don't leave the studio until you get paid.'

We have a special cast float of £500 to pay every extra their daily fee—on the spot.

It not only simplifies the book-keeping but it also keeps them in the studio.

Liaison between the production offices and the writing team is the responsibility of Harvey Higgins. Harvey joined us as Script Associate just over a year ago; he is an ex-schoolteacher and used to present schools programmes for us in the Midlands.

Scripts reach the production office three to four months ahead of when they actually go into production and we are always on the look-out for new young writers who can plan ahead and keep up the pace.

Ian Scrivens, whose name you will see on the screen sometimes in the list of credits, actually started with us when he was at school. At least, he submitted sample scripts when he was at school and is now, at nineteen, one of our team.

Michael Jackson, another youngster writing our scripts, is in his twenties and works in the Promotions' Department of ATV.

Scripts that have final approval are typed in the production office by Mercia Bettson, twenty-eight, who has been with us for six years, and Margaret Bannister, twenty-nine, who joined us earlier this year.

Both are *Crossroads* fans and although they are the first to know what is going to happen they still go home to watch as many episodes as they can.

'It's fun to see how it all turns out,' says Mercia. 'And of course, we never tell our friends or our families just what lies ahead, though they often try and get us to give them a few hints. Over the years *Crossroads* has developed with more characters and more interests, but the basic idea of

the serial has remained the same. It has become more interesting.'

Our production office is on the fourth floor of our new
Studio Centre in the heart of Birmingham—a bright, airy
room with orange doors and white walls. It overlooks the
newly built Holiday Inn hotel with its swimming pool and
sunbathing patio.

Barbara Plant is in charge of contacting the extras and
engaging them, once Maggie French has outlined her requirements.

There are also two typists who deal with viewers' mail
and these total hundreds of letters a week. Every letter is
answered. I always answer my own mail personally and my
secretary is kept very busy dealing with this aspect of Meg
Richardson's life.

The scripts themselves are only typed once and then are
photocopied. Reg Watson devised a special colour system
in our early days which is still in use: we get four scripts
a week and we have a different colour for each.

The first episode is printed on green foolscap paper, the
second episode on yellow, the third on pink and the final,
fourth script of the week is coloured blue.

Each script of thirty-eight pages covers about ten scenes
and lasts just over twenty minutes on the air. Each scene
lasts about two minutes and the complete script is always
devised to have a mild cliff-hanger, or teaser, half-way
through when the commercial break is introduced, followed
by a much stronger cliff-hanger on which the programme
is faded out—so as to make you all want to tune in again
to see what will happen.

I have told you the schedule for the actual writing and
preparation of the scripts but none of the cast, not even
Meg Richardson, is allowed to attend these script conferences and discussions. This is a strict rule. We are all
kept in the dark as to what is going to happen to us.

This is deliberate. If we knew too far in advance how our
roles would develop we would lose the spontaneity and
surprise reaction that is often so necessary when we have

to live these moments for real in the studio. The fact that none of us is told anything about the plot till the very last moment has had some amusing consequences.

When Gerald Bailey (James Donelly) had been earmarked as the victim of a hit and run driver none of us had any idea as to who was going to die. We knew a death had been arranged but that was all. So we had a raffle among ourselves and whoever drew Gerald Bailey won a few shillings at our first rehearsal when we were handed the scripts containing the victim's name.

As it happened, the person responsible for the death didn't know anything about this either. It came as something of a shock for the actor concerned when he discovered, in his turn, that he was to be the motorist responsible.

Viewers were also having bets among themselves as to the identity of the unknown motorist. One Birmingham publican lost £50.

I can only recall one occasion when one of us was told in advance of a plot development. This was when Mrs Hope's home was to be burned down. Joy Andrews, who played the part, had been buying some new clothes to wear in *Crossroads* and since her entire home was going up in flames, the scriptwriters intended that her clothes would be in ashes too. In fact, it was part of the plot that she should be seen in the same dress for several programmes. Fortunately, Liz Stern, who attends the script conferences as our stage manager, knew what lay ahead so she went to Reg Watson and he agreed that Joy should be told not to buy herself any more new clothes.

'You just won't be needing them,' Liz told her. 'You'll never wear them.'

But in general, none of us see the scripts until about a week before we actually rehearse them. Personally, as I learn lines quickly and easily, I make a habit of never looking at my scripts at all until I turn up on a Monday morning to rehearse that first episode.

Each Monday we meet in rehearsal room in Bradford Street, Birmingham, right next door to a night-club.

This is the moment when newcomers to the cast join us and if they haven't been on the programme before, we make a special point of doing our best to make them feel at home.

Alongside the large, bare rehearsal room, we have a sitting-room with easy chairs, table, and magazines—rather like a doctor's waiting-room. Indeed, that's where we *do* wait until summoned to rehearse.

Liz Stern, our stage manager from the start, shows the newcomers our sitting-room and little kitchen, explaining that they can always make themselves a quick cuppa during the next three days. For this will be their working home until the Wednesday night. The four programmes which we will be recording in the studio are all rehearsed and planned each week by the director at Bradford Street before we get anywhere near the studio.

The duties of our stage manager Liz Stern are, however, rather more than merely welcoming newcomers. Liz is responsible for arranging that we have all the props we need. To do this means she has to read all the scripts well ahead of time and make out a weekly prop list. Every week she attends rehearsals in Bradford Street so that she will be able to let the Props Department know of any further articles we are likely to need.

In addition, Liz is also our continuity girl: she sees that we have the correct time on the clocks which you see on the *Crossroads* set; ensures that the same ornaments are in position in my sitting-room and so on.

My present sitting-room is the third that Meg has had refurnished over the years—just as she might do if it was all for real. But that painting of a vase of flowers over the drink table has remained throughout—it's one of Meg's favourites, and mine too.

Liz Stern came to us from the Alexandra Rep., where she had also been stage manager, along with so many of our original cast.

On Monday, after we are all assembled in the rehearsal rooms, we read through the four episodes and get to know what we have to do. Tuesday is much the same, but on a tighter basis. By then we are all expected to know our lines.

Wednesday, the director runs through all four episodes and we have what is called the Producer's Run. This is staged in the afternoon when the producer comes to see how we are getting on and to make whatever improvements he thinks fit.

On Thursday, at 9.30 a.m., we report to Studio One—our biggest studio in ATV's Studio Centre.

By this time all the sets are in position, the technicians are assembled, and we have what we call a 'Stagger' of the first episode till 11 a.m.

A 'Stagger' is the first studio rehearsal when the director positions his cameras and lighting.

After a half-hour break for make-up and coffee in the canteen, we're back in the studio, now dressed in the clothes in which we will be seen on the programme.

From 11.30 until midday we have the Dress Rehearsal. Another half-hour break, visiting the Make-up Department and so on, and then we tape the first programme. If all goes well, we're finished by 1.30, when we break for lunch.

In any case, we *have* to be finished with this first episode by 1.45 otherwise the whole tight schedule of making four episodes of *Crossroads* a week would be thrown out of gear.

I know many performers joining us for the first time find this routine tough. It *is* tough—at the start. Reg Watson always maintained that much of the success of *Crossroads* is due to the freshness and the spontaneity which we manage to achieve with each episode on the screen.

The secret of this—and I agree completely—is our tight format of making the programme. There is hardly any editing. We do not work on a stop-and-start basis like most TV productions.

Each programme is taped just as it happens. Some performers can't cope with this and then they don't stay in *Crossroads* for very long.

112

No other drama programme in British television is produced on this basis—but then, no other studio is turning out a four-days-a-week serial.

On Thursday afternoon we complete the second programme, on the same basis as the first.

The same procedure follows on Friday and by 8 p.m. on Friday four more *Crossroads* programmes are in the can and we're ready to start all over again on Monday morning.

As far as the bulk of our viewers are concerned and by that I mean all ITV areas except London and Manchester, the programmes reach viewers' screens just two weeks after leaving the studio floor.

It is the director's responsibility to direct and tape the actual programmes; the producer has the overall responsibility for them. So while we are working in the studio on Thursday and Friday, the studio scenes are relayed by closed circuit to the producer's office for him to see what is going on and to enable him to make any changes he considers necessary.

Three studio crews work in rotation every week so each episode involves eight technicians working on cameras; seven on sound; five on Props (looking after the articles and sets we use) plus three more on Wardrobe, which entails looking after the clothes we wear.

In addition, the Make-up Department is involved, together with the studio lighting men and others, to comprise a total of over sixty studio experts working behind the cameras just to bring one *Crossroads* episode to your screens.

As you will realize, it's quite tough going. And I've done this for ten years. Before he left for Australia, so had Reg Watson.

We never use Auto-cues on *Crossroads*. This is a prompting device used by TV news-readers when they deliver news bulletins. A roller is clipped to the side of the camera and this reels off what has to be said, in large easy-to-read print.

The same thing is used in many variety shows and by Eamonn Andrews on *This is Your Life*.

Some performers have cue-boards with their lines chalked on them and held out of vision of the cameras.

Although none of these prompting methods are used on *Crossroads* we do have a prompting device, operated by Liz Stern.

During transmission she sits out of camera range with the script and if any of us dry up and forget our lines she presses a Prompt button which cuts out the sound recording. She then tells us the missing line and we carry on.

This method works smoothly enough but Norman Mitchell, who plays Sergeant Tidmarsh, has managed to improve on this.

He always has his lines pasted inside his police helmet or his notebook. (Memories of Sandy in Tunisia!)

If he forgets them he either takes off his helmet or just adds a few words of his own, such as 'Just a moment, I'll make a note.' And then Sergeant Tidmarsh carries smoothly on.

The right theme music is vital for any long-running TV programme and Reg Watson invited Tony Hatch, one of the most prolific composers in the business, to write our theme for *Crossroads*.

Tony Hatch—with whom I have appeared several times as a panellist on *New Faces*, ATV's Saturday night talent show, is a specialist in this field. He has written TV themes for no less than fourteen series—including *Man Alive, Sports Night, Emmerdale Farm, Hadleigh,* and *Love Story*.

This is in addition to his many successes in the field of pop music—hits like *Downtown* and *Call Me* and others like *Don't Sleep in the Subway* and *I Couldn't Live Without Your Love* which he wrote in partnership with his wife, Jackie Trent, altogether, he has fifteen major song hits to his credit.

Reg got in touch with Tony back in 1964, when the first scripts were being written, gave him a rough outline of the plot, and indicated that some of the action would involve

Meg Richardson and her family at their motel and the other involvement would be Kitty Jarvis, Meg's sister, and her family living in a Birmingham suburb.

Tony came up with two themes, written in counterpoint. One theme was predominated by a twelve-string electric guitar and the other was overshadowed by an oboe.

His original idea was to use, as an introduction, whichever theme was appropriate to the family which was first seen on the screen. A very novel approach.

However, as you now know, the death of Beryl Johnstone caused the whole concept of *Crossroads* to be changed. Miss Tatum and the village post office replaced the shop that Kitty had owned and a whole new dimension was introduced with more characters being invented to create the village life of King's Oak.

With the changing of *Crossroads*, Tony's original idea no longer applied, so today we always use the same short musical introduction to each episode—just seven notes of the main theme.

Tony Hatch tells me it only took him ten minutes to write our *Crossroads* theme music. He sat down at his piano, with a tape recorder, and doodled with the notes.

'It came very quickly,' he admits. 'I was seeking a wistful, dreamy kind of thing. Something quite the opposite to *Coronation Street* with its trumpets. I had seen the first script by then and I wanted a very short motif that people would remember and associate with the programme.

'As this was for family viewing, the music had to be readily identified so that any one of the family hearing it from another room could instantly recognize it and get to the TV set in time to watch.'

Once he had the tune written down he called Reg in Birmingham and the two of them met in London. Tony played the theme over to him—it was only thirty-two bars— and Reg agreed at once that it had just the right impact.

Then came the recording session at ATV's Elstree studios. Tony hired the musicians and arrived with a small orchestra of seven, comprising these instruments: twelve-string electric guitar, oboe, acoustic six-string guitar, piano, bass, drums and—most important of all—a harp.

The harp was needed to provide that unusual ripple effect you hear at the end of every *Crossroads* programme. This, in itself, suggests continuity—that *Crossroads* will be returning to the screen as indeed it has done, over and over again for ten years.

The *Crossroads* theme was recorded in various lengths: two minutes, one minute, thirty seconds and the five to seven seconds sequence with which we open.

The theme is also used when we fade in and out of the commercials, as well as at the beginning and end of each programme. Hence the necessity of having it available to fill both short and long time slots.

That ten minutes work by Tony Hatch at the piano in 1964 has paid off handsomely in royalties. Originally, when our serial wasn't fully networked, the composer's royalty was quite small but now that we are seen throughout Britain and in Australia, Tony estimates it is bringing him in over £2,000 a year.

His *Crossroads* theme has already earned him over £10,000 and it would have been much more if the ITV network had taken the show from the start.

Today, every time you hear the *Crossroads* theme, the man who wrote it is richer by £10.

CHAPTER EIGHT

Over the past ten years, my television motel has prospered and been enlarged—just as it might have in real life.

Although viewers have never seen the whole of the outside of my motel it really does exist—in a rather splendid picture on the wall of our production office.

The Malvern Hills are in the background and you can see the original old house that Meg opened back in 1964. Additional flat-top buildings have been put up around it—the conference room, sixteen chalets, cafeteria, garage, petrol pumps, and our small private airfield.

The grounds now cover several acres and, from the look of that painting, Meg Richardson must have been very successful indeed.

Reg Watson had this picture specially painted by one of our artists. The layout is also included in the 'Crossroads bible' which we give new scriptwriters and directors when they come to work on the programme.

This 'bible' contains all the information necessary about our mythical motel and the characters that come and go through its doors.

It also has the 'do's and don'ts' about writing for us. For example, they are told that telephone calls to someone whom the viewer has never seen will be cut, unless it is known that the call will have some bearing on the story in the future.

Also, the contents of a motel menu are unimportant if they have no relation to the story. But a menu is essential if, for example, the cheese flan mentioned on it has been laced with poison and if this fact is to be used in the story line.

Writers are reminded that dialogue is usually unnecessary where what is *said* can be *seen* by the viewer.

There is no point in Meg saying to someone 'Here's Sandy arriving' if they see Sandy wheeling himself into view. They are warned that, as a general rule, all dialogue must have some bearing on the plot and if it doesn't, then it will be deleted.

Each character has to have his own style of dialogue. Wilf Harvey's words, for instance, would be very different from mine or Sandy's.

Writers also have to indicate the clothes that we are to wear, i.e. street clothes, cocktail frocks, or evening dress. The time of day is essential too. Day or night has to be indicated as well as the approximate time the action takes place.

They are also given guide lines of the Independent Broadcasting Authority's rules governing *Crossroads*. I have already mentioned the ban on cigarette smoking—though pipes and cigars are allowed.

As the programme is seen in some areas during the early afternoon, many of our audience are young children. So although it is the policy of *Crossroads* to introduce some strong stories, it is not our business to thrust the sexual facts of life at them—nor would we wish to do so.

This explains why you will never hear any of our characters talk about 'sleeping around', 'shacking up', and so forth. In addition, all swearing is banned.

Research has shown just how unintended offence can be caused to some viewers when TV scripts use certain terms which, although in use in everyday language, are offensive to certain sections of our audience.

Because of this you will never hear us using the euphemism 'basket' to convey that we really mean the word 'bastard'. Our research department tells us this will offend 8 per cent of our television audience; 'to Welsh' will upset 5·5 per cent—our Welsh viewers in fact, and to say someone got into 'a paddy' will annoy our Irish viewers, who total 4·6 per cent.

We also never use phrases like 'coloured gentleman', 'a black', or 'a Jew'. Instead we settle for 'Negro', 'coloured man', and 'Jewish'. These terms are acceptable to Negro and Jewish viewers—the other versions aren't.

We also ask our scriptwriters to act out certain movements for themselves before putting them on paper for us to carry out.

For example, if drinks are to be ordered at the bar, then the ensuing dialogue must not include any reference to 'cheers', 'down the hatch', or some such expression, until the barman has been given time to mix and serve the drinks and we have all had time to raise our glasses.

The champagne we sometimes drink is always the real stuff. Viewers would soon spot the difference if it wasn't. Champagne cider and even sparkling white wine don't have the same wired corks that you get with champagne bottles. Many of them even have plastic stoppers and that just wouldn't be acceptable in the interests of reality.

If you see a champagne bottle being opened, then it's real, but if someone walks on with a glass, then it's probably cider.

On the rare occasions when a bottle has to be opened in front of the cameras, there is always the danger that the cork will jump out with a loud report and the champagne gush up in the air like a miniature oil well.

If you keep a bottle of champagne under the arc lamps in the studio for a couple of hours during rehearsal the heat is tremendous so whenever possible, any bottle that has to be opened on the set is kept in a refrigerator until the last moment.

We always avoid having anyone seen in vision make a complete dialling of a phone number. The reason being that it can take up to eighteen seconds to dial seven digits; there is a time lag too before a phone call is answered at the other end. If we allowed all this to be seen, the action would be held up for too long.

Speeches must be as simple as possible—for people in real life talk simply and directly. Our writers are also

119

asked to avoid using lines like 'a silly sort of situation'. When spoken, this sounds like a long hiss. In fact, we deliberately instruct them not to use any 'systematically sustained sequence of several similar sibilants'—just to stress what we mean.

This sort of dialogue is not only difficult for an actor to say, it also is quite out of keeping with what is said in everyday situations.

When new characters are introduced they must be made distinctive. Any mannerisms that can be introduced in their speech or gestures are helpful in establishing them as characters not only to the viewers, but also to the performers who are trying to bring them to life in the television studio.

Everyone is warned against using trade names. Martini is never used but anonymous vermouth can be mentioned. We are also on the look-out not to mention Hoover, though vacuum cleaner is permitted.

When business names are used checks have to be made that they don't really exist. Even the names of race-horses have to be cleared as non-existent.

In our early days we had several scenes involving a shady driving school. We needed some outlandish title for the school, something effective but maybe a little bizarre.

The name of the *Pass Quick School of Motoring* was finally chosen. It seemed to have just the right shade of subtle suggestion that, perhaps, all was not quite what it should be.

The title was used on the programme and within a few minutes after we had come off the air we had a phone call of complaint to the studios.

There really was a *Pass Quick School of Motoring* at Wolverhampton and a very respectable firm it was too. After we had explained to the proprieter how we came to choose that name he was kind enough to see the humorous side of the situation. Fortunately, both he and his wife were *Crossroads* fans—so that helped.

120

In one episode one of our writers had a character attribute the attitudes contained in a well known book to the author of that book. But our legal department decided that as the attitudes contained in the book were generally unacceptable to most people, this particular reference could well be libellous, so it was deleted.

All scripts are vetted by ATV's staff lawyers. We also consult the General Medical Council and the National Health Executive Medical Council in Birmingham on all questions involving medical etiquette.

In addition, we have our own medical advisers. When we received letters criticising Sandy's condition and behaviour following his spinal injury, we passed them all over to one of our medical advisers and he wrote back to each person assuring them that, in terms of medical history and behaviour, we were factually correct.

Sometimes voices are heard out of vision. For example, you might hear me calling Amy Turtle before I actually appear on the screen. On these occasions, the scriptwriters insert 'OOV' in front of the dialogue to indicate that the words are said Out of Vision.

When the words are supposed to be coming from radios or television sets, or over the telephone, then we use the word 'DISTORT' on the scripts to indicate this.

The scriptwriting team is also given the birthdates of all our principal make-believe folk, together with their horoscopes. This sometimes helps them to assess their characters and to give them certain characteristics in accordance with their horoscopes.

Since they are creating a life for us in and around the fictitious village of King's Oak, we have prepared for them a potted history of the place.

King's Oak, you may like to know, used to be known as Slohtran ford, marshy ford, and was originally associated with forestry. The first foresters' cottages were built by the river Slotter at the natural point where it was easiest to ford across.

The name—King's Oak—comes from the Civil War when

King Charles hid there for a night, using a giant oak in which to shelter.

Because of the way the river runs through that particular part of the Midlands, plus the lack of bridges, travellers from Stratford to Birmingham have continually by-passed the village. But the track they used has now become the main road on which Meg Richardson's motel stands today.

King's Oak has about seven hundred and fifty villagers and its own Rural District Council. The village has its own police house in which the sergeant lives. He also uses his front room as his combined office and police station.

There are three pubs, one cinema, a railway station, a sub-post office, some shops, and two churches. One of these is a Church of England (St Lawrence's) and the other, a Methodist chapel. The Catholic church is at Heathbury, a small industrial town three miles away.

As Castlewich, five miles to the west of King's Oak, they have a weekly newspaper called the *Castlewich Clarion*.

It is against this background that Meg has existed these past years. It has become very real to her, just as it must have done for all the others whose TV lives have centred on this fictitious part of the Midlands.

We even have maps to show where various regulars are supposed to be living; the position of the *Running Stag* and the other two pubs *The King's Oak* and *The Crown*.

To us they have become real places, as to many of you we have become real people. We have to believe in ourselves and in our surroundings—at least, whenever we are before the cameras.

In my mind's eye, I could take any one of you on a tour of the motel that I run—with its sixteen chalets, swimming pool, and restaurant.

I could show you my sitting-room, office, bedroom. They exist for me as they exist for you, even if they are, in reality, just studio sets.

We have our own switchboard at the motel and our own King's Oak telephone numbers. These same fake numbers have to be used whenever phone calls are made, otherwise observant viewers would note our errors.

Writers are told that our terms for an overnight stay are £5.50 per person, payable in advance, and that guests leave luggage in their cars before entering reception. Only newcomers have to be taken to their chalets.

There are also several 'do's and don'ts' which have to be observed in the kitchen—for purposes of hygiene.

No one ever dries a dish with a tea cloth—they are all drip dried. And you will never see any of the kitchen staff washing their hands there—they have to use the washrooms.

Vegetables are never prepared while other food is being cooked and you will never see anyone cleaning floors, ovens, cutlery, or anything like that, while food is being prepared or cooked.

No one can get a drink at the bar in Reception after 10.30 p.m., although residents can be served from a stock kept separate from the bar. This is to conform with the licensing laws. We also have a list of bar prices which have to be changed from time to time, just as they fluctuate in other hotels and pubs.

The writing team have also been supplied with my family tree, showing the various relationships which the Richardson family have with each other.

There is also a potted biography on each individual character, giving their age, education, job, personality and so on.

Here is what the writers are told about Meg Richardson:

MRS MEG RICHARDSON (played by Noele Gordon) 47

Married in May 1969 to Malcolm Ryder. By her previous husband, Charles Richardson, who died in 1961, she has two children: Sandy and Jill. She also has a ward: Bruce Sorbell. See family tree in these Notes.

Board School in Scotland. In her teens, attended an art school (where she met Charles Richardson, also a student).

Managing Director of 'Crossroads' Motel Limited. After

the death of her first husband, she started the motel (it opened on 17th April 1963), and initially was sole owner. But Mrs Hope and Mr Lovejoy each bought a one-third interest in the motel when Meg invested a considerable amount of money in a new venture set up by Malcolm Ryder (she also needed money for the Millstone cottage). Lives at the motel. Has a private sitting-room on ground floor, and bedroom above.

Practical Scots business woman (but no Scots accent). Has a very warm and sympathetic side to her nature. A good 'pawky' humour which she needs in her business. Vast reserves of courage and a youthful outlook, without being self-conscious about it. A proud, bonnie woman. Likes gardening when she has time (she has a private garden in the motel grounds, straight off her living-room); once learnt to fly light aircraft.

Has a car, but owing to her accident which put Vince Parker in hospital is disqualified until early 1970 (she spent some weeks in prison, but the prison sentence was quashed on appeal).

Meg has had at least three suitors since the serial started, including Hugh Mortimer (a local business tycoon; they actually became engaged once, but business problems caused Hugh to go to Australia where he married a younger woman); Kevin McArthur, whom Meg met in Spain (they are still good friends; he acted as motel manager for a time, then later ran a yacht club in Poole); and Malcolm Ryder.

By contrast, here are personal details of Amy Turtle.

MRS AMY TURTLE (played by Ann George)
65
Widow
Village school
Cleaner at *Crossroads* Motel, but also helps prepare vegetables in the kitchen and even waits at tables very occasionally.

Lives in a cottage in the village. She is proud of her cottage.

A born 'stirrer', she has no tact to speak of and the drama of the moment is far more important than the possible outcome of her indiscretion to her. She has to be first with the news, which she hopes will be bad because that's more exciting and gossip-worthy. Interested in spiritualism, and thereby keeps in touch with her late husband Fred. She even consults him on matters of domestic importance, colour of the new curtains, etc., and happily Fred usually comes up with the answer most similar to her own point of view on the subject. High point of her life was a holiday in Tunisia, where Malcolm Ryder treated her royally. Apart from Tunisia, which she remembers with fond affection, everywhere else beyond her immediate surroundings is alien and not to be trusted. Birmingham is a big wicked city rarely if ever visited by her, and London, New York, and Sydney are sort of all one place a long, long way away.

Amy is an English peasant. Her vocabulary is less than that of basic English. In other times, she'd have been the first one out with her knitting needles to watch the guillotine at work.

So as you see, with this kind of information about us all, any writer new to the series can tell at once the kind of people we are and write suitable material for us.

All this goes to show the thoroughness of the research which goes on all the time. First to bring *Crossroads* to life on the screen and then to ensure that it stays vital, interesting, and authentic.

Once the scripts have been prepared, the designers move in. The sets you see in *Crossroads* are all made in our own studios after being planned and designed by our Design Department.

Bearded Rex Spencer, who used to design the annual pantomime décor for the Alexandra Theatre and who has been with ATV since June 1955, when we first started establishing our Midlands operation, heads this section.

Some months before we started *Crossroads*, Reg Watson told Rex of his project. At that time the BBC had a twice-weekly serial called *Compact* which as I have explained, had also been devised by Peter Ling and Hazel Adair who created *Crossroads*.

In planning the production of a daily serial it was essential for our designers to know just how big the sets could be; how they could be prepared for easy dismantling and exactly how they could be fitted into the studio floor space available to allow for the free passage of the camera teams and other technicians, as well as the actors themselves.

Since the BBC had obviously solved all these problems and were coping admirably, it was agreed that the best way to find out how it was all done would be to see it all happening in the BBC's own studios.

Unknown to the BBC, Rex Spencer and Reg Watson visited the *Compact* set, in the company of Peter Ling and Hazel Adair, to do a little private spying on our behalf.

Peter and Hazel took them along as friends to see *Compact* being produced, without telling anyone at the BBC who they really were.

This particular piece of TV spying—saucy though it was —was of tremendous assistance to Rex and his designers and to this day, the BBC have no idea how useful they were in the preparation of our original *Crossroads* sets and backgrounds.

Six sets for simultaneous use, had to be designed to fit into our old studios at Aston Road. First the area they would occupy was taped out on the studio floor and then the sets themselves were designed and built to the available measurements.

Originally Rex designed the motel, which included Meg's suite, the reception area, and the kitchen. Elizabeth Dorrity, another ATV designer, created Kitty's shop, the pub, and other backgrounds.

When we first started our motel it wasn't licensed, so

there was no bar. This came later and was added to the reception area. Hoteliers sometimes criticize us for this, pointing out that no hotel would have its kitchen and bar so close to the reception. Nor would there ever be a sliding door to the kitchen; swing-to doors would operate.

But *Crossroads* began in Meg's private house and we have kept everything just as it was when she began. Of course, if you were building a modern motel today, then the layout would be quite different.

Those early sets of ours were very limited compared with those used today because the studio space available was much smaller. With our new Studio One at Birmingham, we can now have up to eight sets on the studio floor and as they're bigger, this not only gives us all much more room in which to move about but they also allow more performers to take part in the various scenes.

Soon after his sneak visit to the BBC, Rex heard of a new motel opening at Nuneaton, Leicestershire, so he went along there as well, to get some idea of the layout of a motel.

A staff photographer was despatched round the Midlands countryside, taking pictures of rural scenes. These were brought back, blown up, and used as backgrounds outside the fake studio windows. You may not be seeing real Warwickshire country, but, at least, you're seeing the next best thing.

Our Aston studios had been built out of a former cinema and theatre and at the back of what had been the stage, there were huge dock doors to enable scenery and props to be brought in from the street.

This meant, unlike a TV studio, we could drive a motor car right into the studio. Horses could be brought in too, without any difficulty and some of our early *Crossroads* programmes were a cross between a motor show and an agricultural fair.

Rex Spencer and his staff see all the scripts and story lines as soon as they are available so that they can start work on the appropriate sets.

In the ten years they have been working on the programme, they have had to provide over five hundred sets covering such varied scenes as a woman's prison; transport cafés; Tunisian villas; police stations; church weddings, and saloon bars—quite apart from the motel itself.

They must also provide the right background for the right character. For example, if the script shows we are having a wealthy man in the plot and there is to be a scene in his home, then the designers must know all about his social background and character.

If he is plainly a man of little taste, then he gets the room he deserves.

Furnishings are important too—especially with colour TV. Our designers have to ensure that the colours blend and that no particular object, such as a lamp or a cushion, will distract the viewer's gaze from what is happening on the screen.

Originally, Meg's husband was a cartoonist on the *Birmingham Post*, and the house she inherited was a genuine Georgian home—which she turned into a motel.

I'm happy that Rex and his team provided me with such a warm, comfortable background and furnished it all so well. I couldn't have done better myself.

Many viewers must approve too, for every week we get letters asking for details of the furniture and furnishings used in Meg's sitting-room.

They also want the same wallpaper and we've had thousands of enquiries about the floral painting which has been in my sitting-room since the start. It's an original and no one quite knows who painted it or where it came from, but we do pass on details of similar paintings and where they can be obtained.

The alcoves in Meg's sitting-room particularly attract enquiries. They were made in our scenic department and were quite costly, but there is a firm that makes them in fibreglass for about £30 and again, this information is given to the people who write in.

'We want our sitting-room to be just like Meg's,' they tell

Noele Gordon receives a big hug from ex-producer Reg Watson

Tania Robinson and Roger Tonge—two of the members of the
Crossroads 'family'

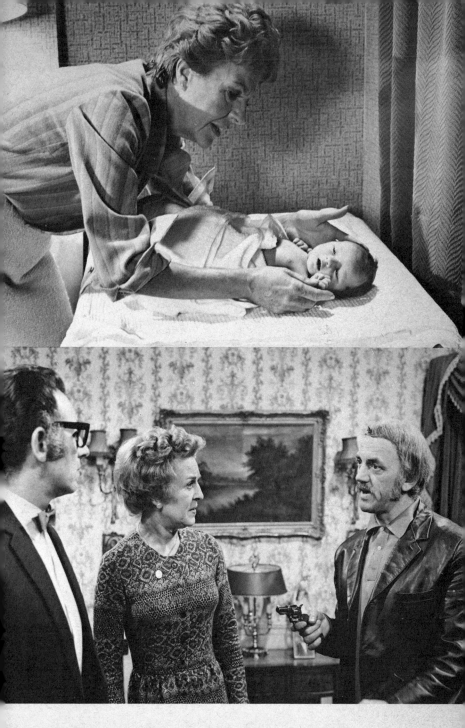

Noele Gordon casts a caring eye over the newest arrival on the
Kings Oak scene, a baby born to Sheila Harvey (Sonia Fox)

(*From left to right*) David Lawton, Joy Andrews and Stan Stennett
in a scene from *Crossroads*

Some trouble at the motel? (*From left to right*) Jane Rossington, Christopher Douglas, Sally Adcock, Ann George and Noele Gordon discuss the problem

The *Crossroads* Cast

The cast celebrating the 1,500th performance with Godfrey Winn

Noele Gordon and Larry Grayson making a guest appearance
in *Crossroads*

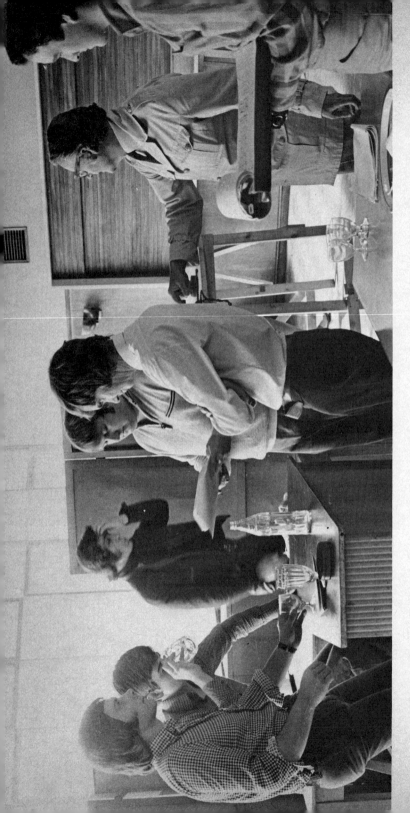

(*From left to right*) David Fennell, Richard Frost, Albert Shepherd, Keith Lascelles (Floor Manager), Reg Watson (Producer), Jack Barton (Director), Christopher Kay (Asst. Floor Manager) at a *Crossroads* rehearsal

me in their letters. This room, in fact, has now been copied in hundreds of viewers' homes throughout Britain.

It must be an odd feeling for them to be sitting in their own lounge and see Meg moving around against the identical background on their television screen.

CHAPTER NINE

Roger Tonge, who is my TV son Sandy, has been with us since we started. He was then an eighteen-year-old playing a boy of fourteen. Now, ten years later, we're not quite sure what age Sandy is supposed to be!

Roger himself is something of a phenomenon. He has changed very little over the years. He has that same foggy croak in his voice that he had when he was supposed to be a fourteen-year-old; it always sounds as if his voice is breaking. But it never does. He still looks a youngster and he doesn't seem to have put on any weight. He's still the same height and for the role of Sandy he is ideal. He even has the same colouring that I have as his TV Mum—red hair, blue eyes.

But although in himself he has changed so little over the years there is no doubt that *Crossroads* has changed his whole way of life.

Roger Tonge today is just about the most successful young actor in British television: in regular work, financially secure, and able to afford some of life's luxuries. He has a Triumph car, colour TV, Hi-Fi, and is talking of buying a new house for his parents with whom he still lives. But curiously enough, he is not all that interested in clothes and has only one suit.

Roger has a number of girlfriends and gets many fan letters from teenagers—especially schoolgirls.

No other young actor playing the role of a TV juvenile can equal the position he holds. As Sandy, he is Britain's best known boy TV star, known to millions.

Roger says he just plays the part as he's always played it —and I'm sure I do the same as his mother. As we've grown older then the characters we're playing have aged at the same time. It just happens. We don't have to think about it.

Roger had always wanted to be an actor. He was an £8-a-week clerk at the Birmingham Post Office and he joined their Post Office Dramatic Society, but they never gave him a part to play and he had to be content with helping backstage.

Every Tuesday evening he went to the Birmingham Theatre School as he could only afford one drama lesson a week. He had only attended six classes, at which he was told he hadn't much future as an actor as he couldn't speak lines, when the *Birmingham Mail* ran an article saying we were looking for a young Birmingham boy to play the role of Sandy.

Some five hundred boy actors had been auditioned but we still hadn't found the right boy for the job. Roger's father, a foodstuffs chemist, saw the article and suggested that Roger should try for the part.

'You've always wanted to be an actor,' he told him, 'now's your chance.'

So Roger phoned the studios and was told to send in a picture with some personal details. In his lunch-hour he went to spend half-a-crown in a photo booth but the pictures were so bad he decided he would stand a better chance if he applied in person.

He came to our studios that evening after he had finished work, showed a cleaner the newspaper cutting, and asked where to go. He caught Maggie French, our production manager, just as she was leaving—she was actually putting on her coat.

Maggie was somewhat surprised to see him. Actors just don't turn up at TV studios looking for work but, as a reward for his cheek, she gave him a script and told him to learn it overnight.

"If you know your lines by then, I'll audition you,' she said.

'I can only come in my lunch-hour,' said Roger.

'That's all right,' said Maggie. 'We'll be here.'

When Roger arrived at the studio the next day the corridors were crammed with boy actors being auditioned and he was asked by Reg Watson to come back in the afternoon for a camera test. Roger explained he couldn't get the afternoon off from work so he went back to the Post Office and arranged to take a half-day out of his fortnight's holiday.

He passed the camera test and finally, Reg whittled down the applicants to just a couple—Roger and another boy.

Knowing what was ahead for them he gave each of the boys the same final test.

'Your pet dog has been run over,' he told them. 'Now just show me how you would react.'

The other boy burst into tears—and said nothing.

But Roger just kept talking—making everything up as he went along.

Since we were about to produce a daily serial which required each and every actor to be able to extemporise at a moment's notice there was no doubt in Reg Watson's mind as to which boy should have the part—Roger.

At the end of his first week his pay packet was £59. 'Untold wealth when I'd only been getting £8,' he says.

For some months now Roger has been appearing on the show in a wheel-chair—crippled by a car crash. No one seems to know whether he will get better or not but the truth, our medical advisers tell us, is that no one with a broken back could ever walk unaided again.

This can only mean that as far as *Crossroads* is concerned Roger Tonge will never walk again either except with callipers and crutches.

All this is in keeping with our *Crossroads* policy—for Sandy is now living a normal life at the motel as Meg's assistant manager. We have shown that, although crippled with a broken back, he can still enjoy many of the good things in life and become a useful member of the community.

This in itself has been a great encouragement to others who have become physically disabled—not only to them

132

personally, but also their families and friends. We have had many letters from viewers supporting us in this. One of them came from the Welsh Disabled Motorists' Club who wrote to congratulate us that unlike many other TV serials we had not made the mistake of giving Sandy a miraculous cure.

'In this situation alone, many problems of the disabled have been highlighted in *Crossroads*,' wrote a club official. 'These include driving, access, financial problems, constant attendance, personal relationships, employment, and so on.

'The accuracy of some of the lines relating to the situations is uncanny; in real life I have either said them myself or have heard them uttered by others.

'The introduction of other physically handicapped people into the serial, the competitive spirits in mentioned sports, have been so close to reality.

'Congratulations—and particularly to Roger for his excellent portrayal of Sandy in this predicament; to the remainder of the cast—their reactions are very real.'

We know from similar responses that come from other organizations that they welcome the way in which we present such matters. They approve and give us all the practical help they can for they recognize we are tackling such situations in a way no other television programme has ever attempted.

For although we are essentially an entertainment programme, our policy is to provide serious information on social matters of importance.

When Roger was first injured he had thousands of 'Get Well' cards sent to him at the studios. He had to lie in a hospital bed, bandaged from head to foot. First of all he was in a coma so this meant he didn't have to say anything and no lines to learn.

The make-up people used to sprinkle glycerine on his face so as to make it appear that his features were covered with sweat. This used to get into his nose and irritate it—but he could never scratch himself on transmission as he was supposed to be paralysed. Whenever I passed the foot of his bed at rehearsals it became a ritual to give his feet a tickle—everyone else did the same.

So all in all, poor Roger spent quite a tortuous time as the victim of a road accident.

It was during this period that one of his fans sent him a record token and he went into the record department of Rackhams, a big Birmingham store, to choose a record. He picked the cover he wanted and took it up to the girl assistant behind the counter.

The girl took one look at Roger and fainted.

'I thought you were paralysed,' she said, just before she passed out.

Roger managed to bring her round and explained that as far as *Crossroads* was concerned he was only acting.

He had another amusing incident at the same store when he went along to buy a brief-case as a leaving present for Reg Watson, together with other members of the cast.

He was standing at the counter when he felt something nipping at his left leg. He thought it must be a dog. Looking down, he saw a middle-aged man on his hands and knees pinching his calf!

An astonished Roger watched as the man went from one leg to the other pinching each in turn.

Then without saying a word, the man stood up and said to his wife, 'It's all right, Mary—they're real,' and off the couple went—satisfied that Roger wasn't paralysed.

I suppose in a way we are to blame here. For when Roger appeared in my *This is Your Life* programme Reg Watson insisted he should stay in his wheel-chair because that's how viewers are seeing him in *Crossroads* and he wanted him to remain in character—paralysed.

Roger has been involved in a couple of fires in the studio during transmission but he managed to cope with both of them—he wasn't in a wheel-chair then. In the first of these I was also involved. We were both in the kitchen with Carlos (Tony Moreton) toasting bread in the toaster and while we were saying our lines Roger noticed that the toaster had caught fire and that flames were coming out of the machine.

He was the only one facing the toaster so neither Tony nor I had any idea why he was pulling such agonized faces at us. However, I turned towards the toaster just in time to see what was happening.

'Put it out, Sandy,' I told him.

We all swung into action, still acting the scene and saying the lines we were supposed to say as we coped with the flaming toaster. When this edition was shown everyone thought that the fire sequence had been intentional.

The other occasion involved an incident aboard Vera's boat. Sandy was there with Margaret Lake who had the role of his girlfriend Liz Clarke and whom he would have been married to if he hadn't had that car crash. In the middle of their scene together Margaret, who was drying some cups, put the tea cloth down on the stove. The gas ring was still alight and the cloth went up in flames. Between them they managed to get the fire under control and to make suitable *ad lib* remarks to fit in with what they were doing.

The director at the time not only covered the whole incident with his cameras but he also gave instructions to the floor manager as to what he should do if the whole set went up in flames.

'Evacuate the studio,' he said, 'but keep one camera on Roger and Margaret—just for the "Midlands News".'

Roger is a natural actor; he has the right outlook and temperament while his croaky Midlands voice is exactly right for a boy brought up with a Midlands background. But in his early days with us there were moments when Reg Watson and I had to be firm with him. On these occasions I really did feel that I was bringing up a youngster of my own.

One of the problems we had with Roger was to get him to have his hair cut. Fashions have changed since then but at that time, when he was just a schoolboy, his long and untidy hair was quite out of keeping as Meg's young son.

After repeated requests Roger still hadn't been to the hairdressers so Reg had a scene written into the script where Jane Rossington, playing my daughter, put Roger into a chair and the two of us went to work to tidy him up. 'Don't take too much off,' he pleaded—and I promised we wouldn't.

At rehearsals I just pretended to give him a haircut but on the actual recording I cut a tiny piece from the back of his head so that he really felt the scissors in action. Now unknown to our victim, Reg had given me a bunch of hair that matched Roger's hair perfectly. I had this hidden behind his back and after that first snip I showed him the handful of hair.

'You're much better off without that lot, my lad,' I told him.

Roger spluttered and went white. He really thought I had cut off most of his hair but he carried through with the scene to the end and it wasn't until he went to a mirror afterwards that he realized we had played a joke on him.

Nevertheless, when he came to the studio the next morning, his hair was neatly trimmed. He had finally got the message!

Roger was also involved with Reg in a slight argument over playing the violin.

Reg told him he wanted him to play the violin for one of our Christmas programmes; I was to sing the old ballad *An Old Violin*, with Roger to accompany me, at the annual *Crossroads* Christmas party.

'But I can't play the violin,' protested Roger.

'I know,' said Reg, 'I've booked lessons for you. You start ten o'clock on Monday morning.'

The following Monday Roger went to the violin teacher and the man just threw up his hands in horror.

'Teach you to play the violin in two weeks—impossible!' he told him.

Even so, Roger manfully struggled through the lessons— but by the end of the week he had made no progress whatsoever.

To make matters worse, every time Reg Watson saw him he always asked, 'How are the violin lessons going, Roger?'

Poor Roger didn't know what to tell him.

That Saturday one of the girl production assistants was getting married and Roger went to the wedding. At the reception afterwards it so happened that a gipsy violinist had been engaged to move among the guests playing various romantic airs.

Roger took the man on one side, told him his problem, and asked if he could teach him to play the violin—in just seven days.

'Well, not exactly teach me to play,' added Roger. 'I only have to learn one tune—do you know *An Old Violin*?'

'You mean—this one?' enquired the violinist and promptly played it for Roger.

'That's the one,' said Roger, 'just show me where I put my fingers, that's all I need.'

The violinist showed him and by the end of the week Roger was playing *An Old Violin*. He played it on the programme. I sang the ballad. And everything went off fine.

In 1967 there was something of a shake-up in the cast and among those who went was Roger. As far as the story line was concerned he was supposed to be emigrating to Canada to make a career for himself as a journalist.

While he was out of *Crossroads* he made a documentary recruitment film for the Navy, appeared in some stage plays in the provinces, and had the part of Hylda Baker's nephew in an episode of *Nearest and Dearest* for Thames TV.

Then he was brought back into the programme for five weeks and when this stint was finished Reg tapped him on the shoulder as he was leaving the studio and asked him if he would like to return on a more permanent basis. This was four years ago.

Meantime, we had moved from our old Aston Road studios to our new ATV Studio Centre in the heart of Birmingham and Roger was due to tape his first programme on the day the studios were being officially opened by Princess Alexandra.

The whole area had been sealed off, crowds lined the streets, and the police were everywhere.

No one had told Roger about this but he found an unguarded back entrance and was able to get into the building only to be greeted by a worried receptionist.

'Reg Watson wants you on the set at once,' she told him.

Roger hurried down to the *Crossroads* studio to find us all lined up.

Reg pushed him into position beside me just in time for him to be presented to Princess Alexandra. The Princess chatted to us both and then continued with her tour of the studio.

'Golly,' whispered Roger, 'I didn't realize you were going to all this trouble—just to welcome me back on *Crossroads*.'

He was serious, too!

CHAPTER TEN

The one man in Meg's life has always been Hugh Mortimer, played by John Bentley.

Hugh was Meg's first big romance after she was widowed and everyone hoped that although he had gone off to Australia he would be returning to marry her.

When he first came to *Crossroads* John Bentley was already well known to viewers for his film appearances as well as for his leading role as the white hunter in thirty-nine episodes of *African Patrol*, filmed on location and shown on ITV.

Originally the role of Hugh Mortimer was that of rather a shady character but with his good looks and charm, he became so popular with viewers we had to make him a hero.

I first met John when he came on to a chat show I used to have with Birmingham journalist and scriptwriter Ivor Jay. It was called *Midlands Profile* and as John is a Midlander— he was born at Sparkhill and made his first broadcast from the Midlands as an actor and singer when he was sixteen— he was an ideal local personality to have on the programme.

Some while later, after *Crossroads* had been running a few months, it was decided to bring a little love interest into Meg's life.

A number of actors were suggested but none of them seemed really right—except John Bentley. Reg Watson offered him the part and I was thrilled when he accepted.

John and I have developed what I think is a somewhat rare and unusual understanding between performers. As an actress, I have never quite found this with anyone else. But the truth is that he has only to look at me and I just melt. He can bring tears to my eyes with just a glance. We have a mutual trust and respect for each other that goes far beyond the normal working partnership between an actor and an actress in a long-running show.

I know his moods and his mannerisms, just as he knows mine. We are a perfect professional team. This kind of combination is, believe me, most unusual in television.

I'm not in love with him—or anything like that—and I'm quite sure that although we have been friends for years, he has no real romantic feelings for me, other than those given him by our scriptwriters. But the fact that we enjoy each other's company, and delight in working together, has brought Meg and Hugh much closer together on the television screen than if the roles were being played by two other performers.

The viewers benefit by this real-life closeness of ours, for television is the one medium that demands sincerity and truth from those appearing on it.

It has never been difficult for me to play a love scene with John Bentley ...

Take that voice of his—it really is a most beautiful, manly sound. The perfect voice for an actor—deep-toned, resonant, meaningful.

It was John's voice that got him his first broadcast—from Martyn C. Webster, the famous BBC radio drama producer, back in the thirties.

This was in radio's hey-day. Mr Webster had just come to Birmingham from Glasgow to organize musical and dramatic programmes from the BBC's Midlands studios.

There were hardly any Midlands actors and actresses around in those days, so he put an advertisement in the *Birmingham Mail* offering to audition any would-be radio performers.

John had never been on a stage before but on his mother's suggestion, he took along a record of the music of *Nymph Errant*. He knew the words of one of the songs from the show—*Experiment*—and used to sing it around the house.

At the BBC's studios he produced the record and asked

140

if they had a gramophone. A sound engineer went into the basement and produced an old style gramophone, complete with horn.

'There you are, young man,' he said. 'But you'll have to wind it yourself.'

John wound up the gramophone, played the record, and sang. Martyn Webster gave him a big role in a large-scale musical in which he was not only the joint lead but also had to sing two solo songs, two duets, and join in a quartet—all backed by the BBC Midlands Orchestra and Chorus.

Needless to say, John came through with flying colours and was launched as an actor and singer.

He has since done the usual stint with both the Birmingham and the Alexandra Repertory Companies and has also worked on Radio Luxembourg as an announcer.

Lately he has been playing Samuel Pepys in a radio serial for Capital Radio, one of London's two commercial radio stations, and he also does a lot of broadcasting work for the BBC.

You may also recognize the voice of Meg's boyfriend, from time to time, in commercial advertisements for such products as Super National Petrol, Smokeless Fuel, Timex, and Cadbury's Flake chocolate.

Like the rest of us, John has had his embarrassing moments on the *Crossroads* set.

He was once playing a scene with actor Tony Howard who had the role of a local reporter trying to interview him on his business deals.

The reporter asked several leading questions which annoyed Hugh Mortimer.

'Get out,' he thundered.

The reporter went to the door, tried to open it, but it remained stuck fast.

'Get out, I say,' said John.

Again, the poor fellow tried to open the door, but it wouldn't budge.

So as there was nothing else to do, John left his desk and pushed the door open for him. It swung with a tremendous bang. All the scenery shook as if an earthquake had hit it. *Crossroads* just carried on as usual.

As we had no facilities for cutting and editing the video-tape, the scene remained in the programme just as it had happened in the studio.

Nowadays, we *can* edit and re-shoot, though in practice, because of the tight scheduling involved, this isn't done very often. In any case, Reg Watson always said that he preferred the spontaneity of the unexpected—and he certainly got it, sometimes!

John Bentley was involved in such a spontaneous scene with me when, standing behind me, he had to reply to something I had said.

As it happened, he hadn't heard me say the line so he didn't know whether to speak or not. However, he was well able to cope with the situation.

He just said, 'Could you repeat that, please?'

I thought he had gone a bit haywire but I did as he asked and said the line all over again.

This time he gave me the right response and we carried on.

Now this wasn't just professionalism. It was also true to life. There are many occasions when one person is talking to another and one of them doesn't hear exactly what is being said. It didn't matter in the least that I had to say the same line twice. When the programme was screened it looked and sounded quite natural. Spontaneous, too!

On another occasion, John was in a sequence with an actor in which the two of them were supposed to be drinking a bottle of wine to celebrate something or other and get slowly drunk as they did so.

It went well at rehearsals, but then Reg Watson had the bright idea that the whole scene would be improved if they started with the camera showing two empty bottles of wine and *then* switched to the two actors.

In other words, they were to play the scene as though they were already drunk—and not get drunk as they went along.

To switch all this around and create an entirely new situation after several rehearsals demands a great deal of acting know-how. But the two of them managed it. Our producer was pleased and our audience benefited with the extra dimension which was brought to the incident.

John is also adept at filling in with extra, unscripted dialogue. Once during an actual transmission, just before the take, Reg took him on one side and told him the show was short of a few minutes.

'I'll have Noele in the kitchen,' he said. 'You just go to her and chat her up a bit.'

Now most stage actors would be completely lost in such a situation but John sailed through it as though it had all been scripted and planned beforehand.

He walked into the kitchen, found me cutting up some carrots, and had a long conversation with me about the benefits of eating raw carrots and their health-giving properties.

It wasn't a serious discussion of course, much more of a send-up. We even put in a few jokes which had the studio technicians laughing—so they must have been fairly amusing.

I remember John picking up a piece of carrot, chewing it, and registering, first, disapproval and then approval on his face as he slowly munched away.

A clever little carrot cameo that only an experienced performer could provide at a moment's notice ...

We were once on location in Shropshire and John had to sit on a bank, pretending to be fishing, while he did his best as Hugh Mortimer, to persuade Roger Tonge (Sandy), what a good thing it would be if Meg would marry him—just as he's been doing lately, all over again.

When they came to the end of the script they received a signal from the director to keep going as more material was required.

So instead of a two minutes' chat, the two of them kept talking for a total of twelve minutes. And if you think this is an easy thing to do, then I suggest you try it sometime by putting yourself in the same situation. Just try to act a scene like that and make up the words as you go along. It isn't easy.

I always had the feeling that the role of Hugh Mortimer was created so as to give Meg not only the essential love that every woman needs, but also some kind of security, a man on whose friendship she could depend.

This is how both John and I saw the role of Hugh Mortimer so it was something of a shock to us when, after he had been written out of the serial by sending him away on a business trip to Australia, poor Meg received a letter to say he had married someone else.

Meg's surprise jilting had an immediate impact on John Bentley in real life.

He had had a long run of eighteen months in the serial and wanted to make a change so as to work in other fields. One of these was in cabaret. For on the strength of his fame as Hugh Mortimer in *Crossroads* he had been booked for a couple of nights as a cabaret act in Birmingham and Wolverhampton.

This was really a try-out for John. He had never done cabaret before but the arrangement was that if he went down well, more bookings would follow.

A few days before he was due to make his début he had a phone call, at his home in Sussex, from the man who had booked him.

'Hugh Mortimer's done the dirty on Meg,' he told him. 'You never told me anything about this.'

John didn't know what the man was talking about. He hadn't been watching the programme so he had no idea that, in the plot, I had suddenly received a letter from Hugh, in Australia, saying he had married someone else.

The cabaret promoter wasn't at all pleased with this development.

'They're not going to like this, you know,' he told John. 'I'm not so sure it's a good thing for you to go on now.'

However, John persuaded him that everything would be

all right and he duly arrived at the club, with chauffeur and hired car, to find queues half-way round the block.

He got out of the car, smiled at his fans, and was at once greeted by a roar of anger.

'How could you do this to Meg?' they shouted.

'You're a rotter,' called out someone else.

'Treat her right,' said another.

He had to run the gauntlet of jeers and boos to the stage door. It was just the same with his act. He walked on to boos and cat-calls. He managed to get through it—but only just.

'It was tough going,' John told me afterwards. 'They hated me for what I'd done to you. I tried to explain that I had nothing to do with the story—that I really did love you, both as John Bentley *and* Hugh Mortimer. In the end they calmed down, but I've cancelled any more cabaret dates. I couldn't go through that again—not after jilting Meg Richardson.'

The reaction from viewers was the same. We were getting letters by every post at the studios—all indignant that Meg should be the jilted victim of that smooth-talking Hugh Mortimer.

It was really all too much for Reg Watson. Following a special script conference, they arranged for Hugh to make a flying visit to England to see me for just one episode and explain why he had married another woman.

Between them they came up with a very heartwarming solution: Hugh explained to Meg that the only reason he had married this other woman (Rosalie Ashley) was because she had only three weeks to live.

She was the daughter of a close friend and was the victim of a brain injury. He had gallantly decided to make the last few days of her life as happy as he could—by marrying her.

This episode was a real tear-jerker. John had tears in his eyes—and I wept.

David Fennell, who plays my nephew Brian Jarvis, was in our opening episode and has been in and out of the programme many times.

David started his television career with us when he was twenty-one and has now appeared in something like nine hundred episodes. In between, he has taken part in a number of TV dramas including *War and Peace* for the BBC and *The Ticket* for London Weekend. He has also been in several Dick Emery shows, playing character roles in sketches.

Lately, as a side-line, he has set himself up in business with a friend.

'We're in the commodity business,' he told me the other day. 'Silver, petrol, wheat—you name it. We put buyers in touch with sellers and vice versa. It's all done with personal contacts. We're now negotiating the sale of an executive jet.'

But at heart he remains an actor, and trained in Birmingham, he made a couple of appearances for Reg Watson as a non-speaking extra in the pop show *For Teenagers Only*. One day, while in the ATV canteen he asked Reg if there was any chance of a job in the new daily serial that he had heard about.

Reg, anxious to preserve the secrecy of *Crossroads* at that time, denied any knowledge of the programme but two days later David had a postcard inviting him to audition for a role.

He went along to our old Aston Road studios and found forty other nervous young actors waiting to be interviewed. They were each given a script, sent home to learn it, and returned the next day to perform the monologue in front of cameras.

Reg had written the scene himself and it involved a boy re-visiting the house where he had spent his childhood. It included some very difficult dialogue and Reg admitted later: 'Any actor who could say that could say anything . . .'

No one told David if he had succeeded and it wasn't until buying a Birmingham paper some days later he learned he had been chosen for the role of my nephew.

The paper had secured the list of the cast for our opening programmes and David's name was included. He rang up

146

Reg who confirmed it all—though somewhat reluctantly. Our producer hadn't wanted the Press to know about his serial quite so soon.

David settled into the *Crossroads* routine with the rest of us and soon found that he was getting recognized in the streets of Birmingham.

He was walking along New Street with Tony Morton when a man spotted them both and his face broke into a smile of recognition. He was some yards away and he walked towards them with his hand outstretched in greeting.

But at the moment he reached them his false teeth fell out on the pavement. He insisted on shaking both actors by the hand before picking them up.

David was once involved in a small drama in the studio when, in a scene with Brian Kent playing his father, one of the heavy studio lamps became loose overhead and fell straight between them, missing them by inches.

This was in the days when we couldn't edit videotape so on a signal from the floor manager, both men carried on with the scene as though nothing had happened.

All that viewers heard was a tremendous crash and they saw a blur on the screen as the lamp fell between two very frightened actors.

Since then, Brian Jarvis has been away in a home for alcoholics and when David returned to the programme, after three months' absence, he learned at the first morning of rehearsals that he had been divorced by Janice his TV wife (Carolyn Lyster). As he hadn't been watching *Crossroads* regularly this was the first he knew about it—but he took it very well!

Last year I had a letter from an old friend of mine, Sheila Mathews. Sheila was the star of commercial television's first variety show, *Friday's Girl*, for the old Associated Rediffusion company. She was also resident singer for a long while on my *Lunch Box* show, so when she asked if there was any chance of working in *Crossroads* I went straight to Reg Watson who put her into our *Crossroads* family as Laura Marshall, David Hunter's fiancée.

Within a few days of her *Crossroads* début, Sheila was being stopped in the Birmingham streets by passers-by asking if she was the new Laura they had been seeing on the screen.

'I never had this kind of impact with my stage appearances,' she says.

This is Sheila's first dramatic role on television but she is well known to West End theatregoers for her appearances in musical shows, having starred at the London Palladium with Tommy Trinder in *Happy and Glorious* and appeared with Joe Brown at the Adelphi Theatre in *Charlie Girl*.

Sheila has come to *Crossroads* straight from winning rave notices after taking over Lauren Bacall's role in *Applause*. This must have been a fairly exhausting experience. In one scene Sheila had to change in forty-five seconds flat from evening dress, evening shoes, and so forth, into an entire day outfit. Good training for the pace of *Crossroads*!

Her two daughters, Sally, sixteen, and Jane, thirteen, had to wait six months before they could see their mother on *Crossroads* because of London being six months behind with their transmissions.

'There's just one disadvantage about watching yourself on the screen at home six months later,' says Sheila. 'I'm the only one in our family who knows just what is going to happen, not only to Laura Marshall but to everyone else in the story. But I've promised my girls not to tell them—it would spoil it all if I told them everything beforehand. They'll have to be patient and see for themselves.'

Soon after joining us, Sheila was involved in a scene with Ronnie Allen in which the two of them were cleaning a chimney in David Hunter's cottage.

They were getting it ready prior to having Laura and David's cottage knocked into one, to make a home for them after their marriage.

At the end of the chimney sweeping it had been arranged for a shower of soot to fall on them, so as to introduce some comedy into the situation. As this couldn't be rehearsed beforehand, the actual fall of soot was kept until the final recording.

Ronnie and Sheila knew what was to happen to them—just as we did. But none of us was prepared for the enormous load of muck that our Props Department had assembled in an outsize bucket and placed in the chimney beforehand.

When the moment came to tip the bucket and release it all they were covered from head to toe in a huge shower of soot, oil, and black paint. It was far more than anyone had expected and they stood there, spluttering like a couple of Black and White Minstrels who had been tarred and feathered.

The cameramen, stifling their laughter, continued to cover them and only the whites of their eyes distinguished them as human. It all provided an hilarious ending—real custard-pie comedy, except that it wasn't exactly custard.

As you can imagine, neither Ronnie nor Sheila thought it at all funny. After two showers they still couldn't get the stuff out of their hair and skin. Two make-up girls had to work on them for a couple of hours, creaming off the black, sooty mess. They were in such a state they couldn't go back to London and had to stay overnight.

Their clothes were ruined and they both had to have new outfits—right through to their underwear.

All this—just to give *Crossroads* viewers a few seconds of fun ...

Ronald Allen, thirty-nine, who plays David Hunter, Laura's fiancé, has had more experience of playing in TV soap operas than any of us.

When Ronnie came to us in 1971, he had already spent three and a half years as the owner of a woman's magazine in the BBC's *Compact* serial, followed by seven months as the manager of a football club in another BBC serial *United*.

'I prefer serials to straight plays,' he says. 'Not only do

you get a chance to develop the character you are portraying, but you also get a real sense of involvement with the audience.

'When I've been in plays or made a film, I have enjoyed doing it but once it's done that's the end of it all. You have no contact with the audience and you just find yourself another job.

'With a serial it's quite different. As long as you stay in the programme, portraying the same character, then you become involved with the viewers in *that* character.

'You get letters. You meet people in the street. The whole thing becomes a much more personal business. This is what distinguishes a long-running TV serial from one performance in a play and this is really why I enjoy *Crossroads*.'

Ronnie—a handsome bachelor, standing six feet two inches, and trained at RADA—has a house in South London where he enjoys gardening and collecting antiques. He has a housekeeper to look after him and he comes to Birmingham on Sunday evenings, works on *Crossroads* from Monday morning till Friday evening, and then returns to London.

Originally, in the plot, he was married to a somewhat neurotic woman (Janet Hargreaves) who was also a heavy drinker.

During one of their heated man and wife arguments, Ronnie had to hit her—or at least, pretend to do so. Normally, of course, if a man hits a woman there is an outcry of protest from women viewers but in this case, Ronnie had made himself so liked in the role of David Hunter, when the letters starting coming in they were all supporting him ... 'She got what she deserved,' was the general opinion.

Working on *Crossroads* has brought Ronnie in contact again with Sonia Fox, for the two of them were in the BBC's *Compact* serial in which Sonia had the role of a secretary.

'*Crossroads* is much more demanding than the other two serials,' says Ronnie. 'I'm always in three episodes a week, sometimes four, so it's quite tough at times.'

Carolyn Lyster, who lives in Gloucestershire, is another young actress who started her TV career with us back in 1964.

Carolyn, then in her early twenties, was assistant stage manager at the Alexandra Theatre in Birmingham when she auditioned for the part of Janice Gifford, who later married Brian Jarvis.

She had to play a small scene in front of the cameras at our old Aston Road studios and then it was played back to her. Carolyn was so nervous at seeing herself on television for the first time that she rushed out to the Ladies and was promptly sick. However Reg Watson gave her the role and Carolyn stayed with us for several years.

Since leaving *Crossroads* Carolyn has become quite well known and has appeared in a number of stage productions, including the Chichester Festival and the farce *No Sex Please, We're British* at London's Strand Theatre.

She played an air hostess in Yorkshire TV's series *The Professionals* and also had a spell in *Coronation Street* as Jennifer Swann, the fiancée of Bill Kenwright. Carolyn has also been in a number of ITV commercials, including one for Flash, in which she appears as a young housewife.

Trevor Butler, a seventeen-year-old apprentice at a Streetly, Sutton Coldfield engineering works, is another of our latest recruits. Trevor is following in the footsteps of Roger Tonge, for he, too, saw an article in a Birmingham paper saying we were looking for a young boy actor.

He applied for an audition and was given the role of a teenager, born and bred in Birmingham, whose parents originally came from Jamaica.

Trevor's home background in real life is similar to the situation in which he became involved in *Crossroads*. Our story had a teenager from the West Indies, who had never known any other country but Britain, clashing with his somewhat Victorian father who looked back with nostalgia to the way of life he left behind in his own country.

The father, steeped in the tradition of his own background, just couldn't accept that he now had an English son who wanted to live the English way of life. For his son knew nothing about any other way of life; he felt no ties with the West Indies; he regarded himself as a British citizen and wished to live here on the same basis and as an integral part of the same community to which we all belong.

This is a problem very prevalent among Britain's immigrant parents. We had considerable support from Mr Laurence Innis, one of the IBA's Midlands advisers, who is himself from the West Indies. In fact it was at his suggestion that we included this story line to cover the West Indian community that has now settled in ATV's Midlands area.

They come and go in *Crossroads* . . .

We had Tania Robinson, twenty-seven, playing Kay Foster, who was a friend of Sandy's for a while—until she died of a brain tumour.

Then six months later, Tania came back—as Kay's twin sister, Julie.

We didn't want to have the twins exactly alike, so as we couldn't change Tania's face, we changed her hair. In her first role, Tania had long brown shoulder length hair—her own. But on her return, last Spring, she tucked her own hair inside a short, close cropped wig.

Bryan Mosley, who plays Alf Roberts, the Mayor of Weatherfield in *Coronation Street*, has made several appearances with us in various roles. He fits them in with his *Coronation Street* stints.

Stephen Hancock, another *Coronation Street* regular in the role of Ernest Bishop, has also been with *Crossroads*.

Stephen came to us after two years with the Royal Shakespeare Company both as an actor and deputy musical director. He has had two parts—as Councillor Clewes and Warren Haycraft, and managed to look quite different for both of them!

152

Jack Haig created the role of Archie Gibbs for us. Jack, a veteran comic from the heyday of British music halls, has been seen in many of TV's top comedy shows.

He was also one of the stars in the long-running musical *Canterbury Tales* at the Phoenix Theatre, London.

Television announcer Peter Tomlinson, who is ATV's host on the screen for Midlanders at week-ends, has also appeared in *Crossroads*—as a police officer.

Peter made such a realistic cop that he even fooled the technicians who work in our tele-cine room.

Leaving the *Crossroads* set in his police uniform, he went in there and told them to clear the building because of a bomb scare. None of them recognized him. So they all quit at once. They were half-way down the stairs before Peter called them back ...

Madeline Orr, who plays David Hunter's housekeeper, the redoubtable Mrs Bullock, is an Australian actress who made a number of television appearances in her own country before coming to England to make her TV début with us.

In the original script Mrs Bullock wasn't given a Christian name, so when we all had to sign a greeting card Madeline decided to give herself the name of Bessie ... and that's the signature she put on the card—'Bessie Bullock'.

'It was such a terrible name I thought it just right for the part,' she said afterwards. 'And from then on I've been known as Bessie Bullock.'

Madeline went back to Australia on a visit in the summer so now that *Crossroads* is being screened there she will be able to see some of our adventures in her own country.

Zeph Gladstone—Vera Downend, owner of the hair-dressing salon at Meg's motel—is another *Crossroads* regular.

In the story, she lives on a barge next door to Wilf

Harvey and it was she who befriended Diane when she had her illegitimate baby.

Reg Watson had the idea of bringing in the character of Vera—a reformed tart, warmhearted and easy-going. Reg always had a dramatic leaning towards introducing 'tarts with a heart of gold' and we have had several of them in *Crossroads* over the years.

Between her appearances on the programme Zeph is an 'away from it all girl'. She likes to go on long holidays to exotic places such as the Seychelles and safaris in East Africa.

Sometimes you'll see her on the programme with her Shihtzus—a Chinese version of a Yorkshire terrier. His full name is Horatio Nelson but as this is rather a mouthful he just gets called by his Christian name. He is very sweet and well behaved and always seems to enjoy himself when he's appearing before the cameras.

Fortunately I hardly ever appear in the same scene with Horatio. This is just as well for as any performer will tell you, there are no greater scene stealers than animals and children.

Alton Douglas, the Birmingham comedian who has been seen compering *The Golden Shot* has also worked with us in the role of a lorry driver.

Alton is a warm-up specialist. He gets studio audiences in a happy, responsive mood for such top shows as *New Faces, Up the Workers*, and the Jimmy Tarbuck series.

It was Les Cocks, producer of *The Golden Shot* and now in charge of the talent show *New Faces*, who first gave Alton his chance before the cameras. He put him in charge when the regular compere, Norman Vaughan, was away with a throat infection.

When Alton was with us he was supposed to be a lorry driver who had demolished part of Mrs Bullock's cottage by mistake.

He wore dirty overalls with his face grimed and unshaven. Until then, Les Cocks had only seen him as a sophisticated comedian—in his best stage suit, smart shirt, and tie.

Les saw him outside the *Crossroads* studio, took one look at his unkempt, down-at-heel appearance, and said:

'There you are, Alton. I always said I would make you a star.'

One actress who found her *Crossroads* life complicated her life at home was actress Clare Owen.

Clare appeared as Louise Richmond, who was expecting a baby. In one episode, Louise said she didn't want the child and this at once caused a great emotional upset with her own children at home—four-year-old Simon and three-year-old Griffith.

For Clare, wife of a Birmingham solicitor, was also pregnant in real life and had told both her sons. When they saw their mother on television saying she didn't want her new baby they couldn't understand it was just a line in a script. They thought she was talking about her own family and Clare, who was watching with them, had to explain that she hadn't really meant it—it was just a story she had to tell for the benefit of *Crossroads* viewers.

Another very human real-life episode but in this case a tragic one, involved the young actress Gaynor Lord who in 1971 was badly injured in a road accident involving five cars.

Gaynor had been the cheeky secretary in the BBC's *Compact* serial. After the car crash she spent many months in hospital and was so terribly injured she is still confined to a wheel-chair. At one stage she had completely lost her memory but this has gradually returned.

When Reg Watson heard of Gaynor's sad accident he arranged for a small part to be written into *Crossroads* so that she could join us and get used to working in a TV studio again. She played the part of a fellow patient at the hospital where Sandy was receiving treatment. Apart from appearing on the programme she was also able to give Roger some advice on how to manipulate his chair and to

155

convince viewers that he really had been crippled in a car crash—just as she had been.

At rehearsals and during her subsequent appearances in the studio, it was obvious that Gaynor was finding it very hard and a great strain. She was tense and nervous and when it came to the moment before the actual taping she sat shaking in her chair.

It was a harrowing moment for everyone, especially for Roger seated opposite her. We could do nothing to help. We could only watch—and suffer.

But when the director said 'Cue' and the right light came up on the camera in front of her, the shaking suddenly stopped.

In some miraculous way, Gaynor became a cool, calm professional actress again—and played the part perfectly.

This particular scene had to be taped three times because of technical problems. Each time Gaynor shook like a jelly beforehand but each time that red light came on her, professionalism took over and she completed the scene without a hitch.

No one watching Roger and Gaynor on the screen could have had any idea of the tense drama that had taken place in the studio beforehand—or the ordeal Gaynor had suffered.

But for those of us who watched it, this whole incident of an attractive young girl, only twenty-three, crippled in real life and pluckily playing a similar role before a crowd of technicians in a TV studio, was both poignant and moving.

Few had dry eyes on the *Crossroads* set that day ...

Stratford Johns, the BBC's famed Superintendent Barlow, has never appeared on *Crossroads* but he has some very close connections with us.

Morris Parsons, sixty-seven, who is our Wilf Harvey, is Stratford's father-in-law; while his sixty-five-year-old mother-in-law—whose professional name is Mona Ewins—has also taken part in thirty-one of our programmes as Mrs Alice Loomis, our motel housekeeper. Ken Platt, the

Lancashire comedian, played opposite her as her husband.

This combination of Mr and Mrs Parsons, married forty-three years and both playing character roles in our serial, makes them unique in the world of television. They are not just the only married couple to be appearing together in a television serial, they are, in fact, also TV's Darby and Joan.

Morris is now in his fifth year as Wilf Harvey and although he has been in the theatrical profession all his life he cheerfully admits that—nearing seventy—his part in *Crossroads* is the biggest break he has ever had.

It all began when he was appearing in the pantomime *Robin Hood,* which he had also written and produced, at Lewisham, South London. Pearl Carr and Teddy Johnson were the stars and Morris was the Sheriff of Nottingham.

During the run of the pantomime, Maggie French rang to ask if he could be free for a part in *Crossroads*.

'We've got a new family coming into the programme,' she told him. 'We have the son and daughter but not the dad.'

Morris had been with us some three years before in several episodes—as a bus driver. Maggie also knew him as an experienced character actor who had been in such series as *Z Cars* and *Softly, Softly*. But he also had another claim to TV fame—an early appearance in *Coronation Street* ... 'I was the first drunk to be thrown out of the *Rover's Return*.'

So with this kind of background, Morris was a natural choice to play an ex-miner, born and bred in the Black Country, with a grown-up family.

Morris soon developed his role into an important and integral part of our little *Crossroads* community.

During rehearsals, Reg Watson came up to him and asked if there were any problems.

'Only one,' said Morris. 'How long do you want me for?'

'I don't know yet,' Reg told him. 'Why?'

'Well,' explained Morris, 'I have a regular job each summer—producing plays for the Forbes Russell Theatre

157

Company which plays Butlin's camps. If you want me to stay on with you I'll have to let them know.'

'Give me forty-eight hours,' Reg told him.

Two days later Reg was back in the rehearsal room.

'We will keep your part going till June—is that all right?'

'Fine,' said Morris.

That was in 1970 and he is still going strong as Jill's father-in-law.

In one comedy scene he had to take a bath in front of the sitting-room fire. Then later, he was carried out of the room, still in his bath, into the kitchen.

For a start, Morris put on his flat cloth cap and sat in the bath in swimming trunks, while studio technicians frothed up the hot water with foaming suds.

Morris was also given a newspaper to read but, gradually, as the scene progressed, the suds around him became fewer and fewer so when the moment came for him to be carried off he had to use the newspaper to hide his bathing trunks.

But his troubles were by no means over. He had to stay sitting in his tin bath until the scene was finished as he was still within camera range. By this time the water was stone cold. When it all ended, Morris was blue with cold, his teeth were chattering, and it took a stiff drink to pull him round.

'The part of old crosspatch Wilf Harvey has been just wonderful for me,' he admits. 'It has brought my wife and I happiness and security in our old age—something that very rarely happens to people in this profession.

'I've taken a flat in Birmingham now as my wife was getting very lonely being left in London by herself and we have a whole new way of life in the Midlands.

'My daughter's stage name is Nanette Ryder and she met Stratford in repertory long before he became famous as Barlow on television.

'They have three daughters aged eighteen, sixteen, and five and an eleven-year-old son.

'Peta, the sixteen-year-old, wants to go to drama school

but I don't know that any of the others have shown any great interest in the theatre so far.'

Morris has appeared on BBC TV with his son-in-law as Mr Toddy, the owner of a dockside pub. Barlow questioned Mr Toddy over some crime in the neighbourhood but only a handful of viewers could have known their relationship in real life.

Maybe one of these days we can have Barlow making a guest appearance on *Crossroads*—but I doubt if the BBC would agree ...

'Stratford works much harder than I do,' says Morris. 'I've seen him with one hundred pages of script to learn just for one episode on BBC TV.

'But he's a very good actor and I admire his work very much.'

Last year Stratford Johns appeared in the stage thriller *Who Saw Him Die?* with Lee Montague, in Birmingham prior to its presentation in the West End at the Haymarket Theatre.

Morris went along to the Alexandra Theatre and after the show Stratford asked him what he had thought of the production.

'Great,' said Morris. 'But I think you might improve your first entrance.'

He then made a couple of practical suggestions which Stratford accepted and from then on he made his entrance as Morris had suggested.

Like the rest of us, Morris Parsons is now so firmly established in his TV role that millions of people only think of him as Wilf Harvey.

He is often invited to give talks to pigeon breeders and attend their social functions.

'How are the pigeons, Wilf?' is the usual greeting he receives.

But the truth is—TV's Wilf Harvey has never kept a pigeon in his life ...

Just as I have never run a motel.

CHAPTER ELEVEN

Ann George—our plump little Amy Turtle, barely five feet, who spends most of her time poking into other people's business—joined us soon after we started.

After watching our serial at her home in Smethwick, she decided that although Roger Tonge was providing something of a Midlands' accent, in our original cast of eleven, not one of us talked 'real Brummie'.

So Ann did something about it by writing in and suggesting herself for a role. Amy Turtle couldn't have done better!

Ann—her real name is Snape and she took her late husband's Christian name for her stage name—turned up at our studios and was given a short scene to learn in which she was a customer in the shop run by Kitty Jarvis.

Maggie French auditioned her after an hour's study and then she was brought back again for another test.

'No one had told me how to play the part,' she recalls. 'But I saw that they had "they'm" in the script so I said to myself "This is Brummie talk" and I used a strong Birmingham accent for the whole scene.

'Maggie French was tickled pink. Although *Crossroads* was a Midlands programme they really hadn't anyone with a true local accent, so they gave me this part of a customer going into the shop and buying presents for her seven-year-old son's birthday.'

Ann George duly recorded the scene with Brummie accent and mannerisms. She brought the first comedy touch to *Crossroads*.

Many of the studio staff had been recruited locally and they enjoyed her little cameo so much they gave her a round of applause at the first run through.

160

'The next thing I knew, I had a string of appearances,' says Ann. 'After being a customer in the shop, I was given a job there behind the counter. Then when Kitty Jarvis died, I joined Meg at her motel as the charlady.'

She has certainly done very well for herself since then. A hired car and chauffeur bring her to work and she has bought a car for her married son.

When Ann's grandchildren, Joanne and Vicky, first saw her on television as Amy Turtle, she was sitting with them at her son's home. The little girls were most intrigued.

'How did you get inside that box, Grandma?' asked Vicky.

Ann did her best to explain and then Joanne put another question.

'But why do you have to speak like that?' she asked.

'If I didn't speak like that I wouldn't have the job,' explained our Amy.

Ann has now bought herself a £3,000 caravan at Stourport-on-Severn where she now lives. Previously she used to live at Smethwick but she prefers the countryside, especially at week-ends.

There is another reason why she leaves her Smethwick house furnished but unoccupied—it's haunted.

'It was haunted before my husband died,' says Ann. 'So it has nothing to do with his death there. I am very fond of needlework and often when I was alone, tatting in the sitting-room, I used to hear this whishing noise and feel the rush of a strong wind around me.

'It seemed just as though someone was running round the table and going out into the hall and up the stairs. There were thumps and footsteps too. I could *feel* someone else was there but I could never see anything.

'It didn't frighten me particularly, but when it happened it was always around midnight when I alone in the sitting-room and my husband had gone to bed.

'I used to tell him about it and he told me not to be silly, adding that it must be mice or someone next door.

'But one night he had gone to bed and he heard it all

for himself. He came rushing down the stairs wanting to know who our visitors were.

'When he saw I was alone he had to admit that maybe I had been right after all.

'What price the mice now?' I asked him. Anyway, he never joked about it again and I got quite used to the ghost, really. It was quite a gentle ghost and it never did any harm to anyone.

'But after my husband died and I took up acting again I was never really happy there. For one thing, I found I couldn't concentrate on learning my lines ... I'd just get settled down with the script and those bumps and thuds would start. It's much more peaceful in my caravan and I can learn my lines without being interrupted by any ghosts.'

Ann, sixty-two, was born in Erdington and although she has been entertaining people since she was four, *Crossroads* is her first and only TV programme and is also her first experience of straight acting.

Until she gave up the stage in 1951 to nurse her sick husband, Ann had a flourishing career as a singer—appearing with D'Oyley Carte in their Gilbert and Sullivan productions as well as having leading roles in such musicals as *The Belle of New York* and *The Desert Song*.

Our Amy even sang at the Birmingham Town Hall as a soloist in Handel's *Messiah* and today she has an hour-long cabaret act in which she sings and tells jokes.

Sometimes while waiting to rehearse, we get her to give us some of her cabaret routine and I'm sure she won't mind if I tell you one of her favourite stories. It goes something like this:

There were three fellows in a car—an Englishman, a Scotsman, and an Irishman. They'd all had too much to drink and were stopped by the police.

'What names shall we give?' whispered the Scotsman.

'Do what I do,' replied the Englishman and gave his name as 'F. W. Woolworth'.

The Scotsman came next. He gave his name as 'W. H. Smith'.

162

Then came the turn of the Irishman ...

'Allied Carpets,' he said.

So with this kind of repertoire, don't be surprised if we get Amy Turtle telling a few jokes at our next *Crossroads* Christmas party!

One joke she *did* tell me on the programme caused a mild furore at the time—simply because none of us knew the meaning of what she had said, including Ann herself.

Ivor Jay, our specialist in Black Country matters, had included an old Staffordshire saying in Amy Turtle's dialogue.

She was in a scene where one of our male characters was supposed to be getting rather agitated and Amy was trying to calm him down.

'Don't get your cod in a pucker,' she told him. The line stayed in throughout the rehearsals. When it came to the recording no one said anything, although I did notice several of the technicians were finding it difficult to keep a straight face.

The programme duly went out on the air—and then the letters started arriving.

'Don't get your cod in a pucker' turned out to be an old Staffordshire saying which, translated, means 'Don't get your codpiece twisted up.' It's really the male counterpart to the saying 'Don't get your knickers in a twist.'

For a codpiece is the term for the jockstrap styled garment—usually jewelled—worn by men in Elizabethan times as an accessory to their doublet and hose, to protect their masculinity.

Although the phrase is dying out now, it is still in common usage in Staffordshire, so in the interests of authenticity, Amy Turtle was perfectly entitled to use it as a reprimand. I'm sure she got a few laughs from viewers with it, too.

During our early days, Ann was travelling home from the studios during a Birmingham rush hour and, as there wasn't a seat available, she was strap hanging, crushed up against the other passengers.

A woman looked down at her, turned to her neighbour, and said, 'Isn't she like Amy Turtle?'

'I bet you wish you were,' said the other woman.

'No, I don't wish I was,' Anne told her. 'Because I *am* Amy Turtle.'

The two women looked at her in astonishment. Then, just as she was leaving the bus, a male passenger said to her, 'You were pulling their leg—weren't you?'

So Ann said, 'Well, take another look at me. Do you think I'm Amy Turtle, or not?'

'By golly, you're right,' replied the man. 'You've made my day ... by the way, you didn't write those anonymous letters, did you?'

This was a reference to a situation in which Amy Turtle was suspected of writing some poison-pen letters—but of course she hadn't.

When I had my house at Ross-on-Wye, Ann often came to stay with me at week-ends and help me with the gardening. She is especially fond of Mother's cherry cake.

Mother, on the other hand, is always praising Ann for being able to give up smoking, something I've never succeeded in achieving, following an amusing incident on the *Crossroads* set.

Our technicians were busy dismantling the microphone boom equipment which hangs over our heads, following a rehearsal scene between Amy Turtle and Meg Richardson. They had the whole apparatus stripped down when Ann George, who had left the set, returned to enquire what was happening.

I explained that the equipment was picking up a strange whistle during our scene together and they were trying to trace the cause.

The two of us stood there, beneath the suspended microphone, and waited for them to finish. We started the scene again but the director still wasn't satisfied.

'The whistle's still there,' he called down from the control room.

164

Then suddenly he called back again 'It's gone—who's moved?'

Only the two of us were involved in the scene and the only one who had moved had been Ann.

'Amy Turtle's moved,' I told him. 'That's all.'

It was only then that it suddenly dawned on everyone that the whistle which was being picked up wasn't really a fault in the equipment at all. Nor was it exactly a whistle —it was more of a wheeze. In fact, that's just what it was— Amy Turtle's wheezy chest.

'If that's me they can hear, there's only one thing I can do—I'm giving up smoking,' said Ann.

And she hasn't smoked since.

Albert Shepherd, who plays Don Rogers, one of our two village postmen—who eventually married Pat McKenzie (Lynette Erving) joined us three years ago straight from filming *Secret Ceremony* with Robert Mitchum and Elizabeth Taylor.

Elizabeth Taylor had been a G.I. bride and Albert her G.I. husband. Joe Losey was the director and, for good measure, Mia Farrow played their daughter.

Mia Farrow of course had previously been one of the stalwarts of *Peyton Place*. Before we started to work on *Crossroads* there was a special screening of *Peyton Place* which we all attended.

'We're not copying this,' Reg Watson told us. 'We're going to be very different. But I do want you to see the kind of impact a TV serial like *Peyton Place* can have.'

Albert says that his role with *Crossroads* is strictly confined to the sort of chap whose main interests in life is 'beer and birds'. I think he's right.

I do know that in his first big scene with me he came in by the french windows after a remark I had made on first seeing this young, handsome newcomer working in the village post office.

'Things are looking up!' said Meg.

But young Don Rogers took this as an open invitation to

165

call round, unannounced. and make a pass at me. In this first major scene between us I had to bring him down to earth very smartly and show him that Meg just isn't that kind of woman at all.

Everything went smoothly enough at rehearsals but when it came to the final take, Albert was far better than he had ever been at the run-throughs. He *was* Don Rogers.

This was his first big moment with me in *Crossroads* and he stole the scene.

As soon as he looked at me I sensed somehow that he realized his big moment had arrived and he played it with such tremendous verve and spontaneity that I went up to him afterwards to congratulate him.

'I was terribly nervous,' he told me. 'I was actually trembling when I came off. It was my first scene with you and I was quite terrified.'

As it happened, this particular scene was never shown —for the videotape broke down and we had to go through it all over again.

'It won't be the same,' I warned him. 'It never is. You can't give that kind of performance twice.'

And I was right. We played the scene again but it never achieved the impact and excitement that we had found previously. And we both knew it.

In his role of Don Rogers, Albert has been mellowing over the years and I suppose he has now become quite a likeable character. Even though he didn't turn up for that wedding to Pat McKenzie, they did get married quietly a few days later!

But for that first big scene with me, he had to be an arrogant know-all—out to make Meg Richardson. That's how he played the scene and that's what he was meant to do. All he wanted was to get Meg to bed.

It was my job, in the dialogue, to cut him down to size.

I have already told of my own experiences when the Duke of Edinburgh visited us at the studios. On this same occasion, Prince Philip was in the control box with Reg Watson and other ATV executives while Albert Shepherd and Peter Brookes were rehearsing a scene in the studio, below.

This was our 'stagger' run-through, prior to the dress rehearsal. As Prince Philip was in the studio, Reg had decided to combine the two. After all, it would not have been very interesting for the Royal visitor to have seen us run through the scenes on the usual slow, stop and start procedure.

For this sequence, Albert was supposed to be lying down on a sofa and Peter was to come up to him and say something. It so happened that Peter got his words mixed and gave Albert the wrong lines. If this had been a proper dress rehearsal, or on transmission, Albert would have covered up for him and carried on as though nothing was wrong. But because he thought it was just a 'stagger' rehearsal he didn't bother.

The result was that Albert said nothing at all to help out and deliberately left poor Peter floundering. Peter, somewhat exasperated, managed to whisper under his breath, 'Don't fool around. For God's sake carry on and cover for me. This *is* a dress rehearsal. The Duke Edinburgh is in the control room.'

I don't know exactly what Albert *did* say to cover things up, but he managed something. The rehearsal passed off smoothly and Prince Philip never knew anything had gone wrong.

Albert had many letters from viewers when, in the plot, he turned out something of a philanderer at the expense of Pat McKenzie. He used to show me the letters—mostly angry ones from teenagers. They were quite indignant with the way he was treating Pat.

I hope they are all pleased now that he has settled down with her ...

Peter Brookes plays the part of Vince Parker, the other local postman who also works as a part-time barman in the motel.

Peter, who won a scholarship to RADA, comes from

Coventry and it was his desire to work in the Midlands that resulted in his joining our team.

'Try and get me a job in a Midlands serial,' he told his agent.

At that time the BBC had *United* and we had *Crossroads*. His agent arranged an audition with us and Peter has been part of the team since 1967.

Before coming to us he was with the Old Vic for a year and he also performed in a Shakespeare season in Chicago.

I think what especially endeared Peter to me was the moment when he said 'Ta-Ta, Mrs Richardson'. Until then *Crossroads* had always seemed to be something of a suburban serial—associated with tea parties and tennis tournaments.

Coronation Street covered the workers. *Crossroads* covered the suburbs. Without realizing it, the two serials had become involved in a miniature class war—on the TV screen.

Peter was one of the first to spot this. Most of our characters have to be essentially suburban—because of the setting. If you open up a motel your trade has to come from the reasonably well-to-do middle class.

It was Peter who put a touch of cheekiness into *Crossroads*. I don't know what inspired him, but he broke down the suburban, semi-detached atmosphere.

The 'Ta-Ta, Mrs Richardson' did it. No one had ever spoken to Meg like that before and it wasn't in the script. It was a bit of cheek, but in character, and when he said it I knew at once he was right. There was only one thing to do.

'Ta-Ta, Vince,' I said in reply.

Peter beamed—for as he told me afterwards, he didn't quite know how I would take it. And we've been on that basis ever since.

As a regular, Peter has had to learn to cope with the unexpected.

On his first entrance as the new postman he was to arrive at the local post office and report to Miss Tatum, the postmistress (Elisabeth Croft).

However as he arrived early, the idea was to have the post office still shut. This was intended to provide an added touch of comedy as he battered on the closed door.

Everything was fine at rehearsals but when it came to the recording Peter knocked on the door—and it swung open. He stepped inside to find an astonished postmistress looking at him.

'Ah,' said the new postman, 'you should keep that door locked until you open up.'

This opening line, quite unrehearsed, fitted into the situation and was at once acceptable because it was in context and appeared quite natural.

Only an experienced actor could have coped with such a situation and by experience I mean the kind of experience one gets from the theatre. For when it comes to television, the director is far too busy to teach you anything about *acting*.

He expects you to know all about this. He expects you to have done your apprenticeship in *acting* which is why repertory companies provide such tremendous experience and background knowledge for the young performer.

A TV director can position them before the cameras; he can indicate what emotions they have to register, but he just hasn't the time to show them *how*. This is up to the individual. Those that succeed are those who know their job. It's as simple as that.

I remember another occasion—and there have been hundreds—when sheer professionalism and experience has carried us through an awkward moment.

No director likes to stop and start again when things go wrong, so he is particularly grateful to performers who are able to cope with the unexpected during the actual transmission and carry on regardless.

This time Peter Brookes was involved again—with Heather Canning. Heather, who has been with the Royal Shakespeare Company, had the part of a wealthy guest at the motel and Vince Parker (played by Peter) was attracted to her.

169

In this particular scene, Peter and Heather were supposed to be having an argument and Sue Hanson was on the side of the set waiting to walk in and interrupt them.

As it happened, Sue missed her cue and in fact she never arrived on the set at all.

Peter and Heather, realizing what had happened, carried on talking to each other. Between them, they staged a dramatic little farewell scene all on their own.

The woman guest was supposed to be leaving the motel anyway, so they invented their parting—sad and real. Heather even had tears in her eyes. We all watched them, for as the words came out the whole scene took on a new dimension.

It was sheer improvisation. But very effective. And when the moment was screened on TV later, none of the TV audience could possibly have known that Heather and Peter were living an incident which they themselves were creating as they went along.

But in *Crossroads* this happens all the time.

Last year I played a whole sequence of programmes in which I was suffering from amnesia. As is our custom, the whole subject had been carefully researched and approved by our medical advisers.

But you can imagine my embarrassment when, at the end of a scene with Roger Tonge, I had to say a few words to him and then leave—only I didn't go.

I had quite forgotten! I said what I had to say and just stood there. Roger nodded slightly at the door, just to remind me. I stayed where I was, looking back at him. He nodded again.

Then suddenly I remembered. I grabbed my handbag and left the room. By then it was all too late. The cameras had stopped turning and we had run out of time.

A case of genuine amnesia, on my part!

I hope no one was aware that anything had gone wrong when the scene was screened, although they may have wondered about Roger's twitch.

We once had an actor, playing a police constable, who

forgot his lines and said 'I'm sorry, I've gone'. No one took any notice. But as soon as he had apologized he remembered what he really was supposed to say and carried on as though nothing had happened.

This incident also went out just as it occurred. I saw it on TV while watching with some friends; Roger Tonge watched with his parents. But none of our companions spotted anything wrong.

Another unrehearsed movement involved Elisabeth Croft (Miss Tatum) in a scene in a veterinary surgeon's waiting-room where she had taken her sick cat. Sandy had to arrive with Portia, the Great Dane belonging to David Fennell.

Both animals were kept apart until the actual take—with the intention of avoiding any friction between them. But when the cat saw the dog walk in she went berserk. She scratched Elisabeth's face and tore at her clothes. The cameras continued to turn while Elisabeth just shrieked.

Roger tried to pacify her and attend to her wounds. The only calm creature was the Great Dane. She stood there, quite unmoved, and when the scene was shown it was the dignified Portia who stole it.

Actors can never really compete with animals; they're the greatest scene stealers of all.

Portia was a beautiful creature who used to bound around the set thinking she was a fox-terrier. We all missed her very much when she died.

She was very popular with the viewers too, especially the children. In a classroom at a Birmingham school pupils were sitting for their 'O' Levels and one of the questions was *Who was Portia?*

Every child gave the same answer—'The dog in *Crossroads*!'

Dark-haired Sonia Fox is another *Crossroads* regular. She plays Sheila, the daughter of Wilf Harvey, the pigeon fancier, and is the sister of Stan Harvey who is married to my TV daughter Jill. So Sheila is one of the family.

171

Sonia had been in the original hospital series *Emergency–Ward 10* for two years, as Staff Nurse Amy Williams, before coming to join our life at the motel.

She was also in the BBC's *Compact*, so *Crossroads* is her third TV serial.

Few of you will be aware of this, but Sonia first worked with us about five years ago—in the small role of a kleptomaniac. When we wanted to cast the role of Sheila Harvey, Reg Watson offered her the job.

'No one will remember that you've been in the story before, in another role,' he told her.

And it seems they haven't.

Shelia Harvey provided one of our biggest talking points for women viewers when she found she was pregnant. Her indecision as to whether she would bring up the child herself, have it adopted, or have an abortion, provided many tense and human scenes.

Sonia made such a good job of the role that after the sequence in which she openly talked of having an abortion, a woman spat at her at Birmingham's New Street station, just as she had arrived from London to report at the studios.

'It's a disgusting, terrible thing you're thinking of doing,' the woman screamed at her—in an Irish accent and red with rage.

Sonia later took it as a compliment to her acting, but she was in tears when she told us about it on reaching the studios.

For six months she had to wear a pouch-like contraption underneath her clothes, fastened by two tapes tied at the back, to give viewers the impression that she really was pregnant.

To add to the realism, she added cotton wool to the pouch every week so, as the serial progressed, Sonia got bigger and bigger.

She really *was* carrying, even though it was only cotton wool.

When *Crossroads* first started we would never have been

allowed by the IBA to include this kind of situation in our story line. But things have changed in ten years and we even showed the birth of Sonia's baby on the screen without any protests—from anyone.

It was a deliberate policy decision on Reg Watson's part to present the problems of an unmarried mother and have her talk about abortions or adoptions—just as women in this situation often do. Our whole story line covered the issues confronting a pregnant, unmarried woman and the pressures which face her.

I'm sure it had a much greater impact and made a much bigger contribution to this problem than any documentary. We had many letters from unmarried women awaiting their babies thanking us for the help we had given them with their problem.

The actual birth of Sheila's baby was supposed to take place on the dining-room floor and I acted as midwife—having been shown by Birmingham's Queen Elizabeth Maternity Hospital just what I had to do. This sequence, without the baby being seen, was taped in our studio.

Then I was shown holding the baby immediately after the birth. This was filmed at the hospital and we used Karen Furze, daughter of a Bourneville policeman, Graham Furze, who had been born just a day and a half before.

But as far as the TV audience was concerned, it looked as though the whole scene had taken place at *Crossroads*. After all, you couldn't risk bringing a newly born baby into a television studio—not even for *Crossroads*.

Richard Frost, twenty-seven, is the actor who has the part of Roy Mollison who seduced Sheila Harvey, though he did make amends by marrying her in the end.

Richard, who was trained at the Bristol Old Vic, must be a patient fellow. He waited seven years before getting a part with us! He first went to see Reg Watson in 1966 to ask for a job, but it wasn't until all this time later that a suitable character for him to play was introduced into the plot and

Richard, whose home is in the Midlands, was able to join us.

Just as Sonia Fox suffered for playing the part of an unmarried, pregnant woman considering an abortion, so Richard came in for his share of mild abuse—for getting her into that condition.

One day he came to the studio and said the whole situation had become so embarrassing in his private life that he was beginning to wish he had never come to *Crossroads*.

It seemed that his girlfriend at that time had left him. The scenes in which he was involved with Sonia were upsetting her too much. She couldn't bear the thought that he had not only become involved with any other girl, but in addition, had made her pregnant.

'It was all too much for her,' Richard told me. 'She just couldn't cope with it. All the girls where she worked were making jokes about it and her family didn't think it at all funny. Neither did she—she left me.'

Richard is back with us now, after appearing as Thomas Cromwell in *A Man For All Seasons* at the Playhouse, Salisbury. He has been an actor since he was seventeen, but this was the first time he had ever lost a girlfriend because of any of the roles he played.

I told him to regard it in the same way as Sonia had with the woman who had spat at her—as a tribute to his acting skill. However, right up to the time he married Sheila on television, he came in for a great deal of ribald comment when people recognized him in the street.

'What a naughty boy *you've* been,' they used to say to him. Barmaids would serve him drinks and say, 'Don't think you can treat me like you treated Sheila.'

'I found it a bit embarrassing sometimes,' he admits. 'Especially when other people in the bar didn't realize I was an actor and thought I really had put some girl called Sheila in the family way.'

Richard is another who says he has found working on *Crossroads* something of a challenge. He was telling me the other day about some long scene he had to play with Sonia. They were both doing their best to remember their lines when, suddenly, just before the actual transmission, the director sent them a message.

'Can you do the scene—twice as fast. We're short of time?'

Well somehow they managed it. The scene finished on time and I don't suppose anyone noticed the speed-up. Incidents such as this are very stimulating—a far cry from the normal stage play.

As Richard says, 'It's fun, really. Keeps you on your toes.'

William Avenell, who plays Mr Lovejoy, our head chef, has been with us since April 1968. He is an experienced repertory actor and spent two years with the Shakespeare Memorial Theatre before joining us in the small part of a brush salesman. Then he became a veterinary surgeon and went on to play half a dozen small parts before settling down in his present role. Mr Loveday's Christian name is Gerald, though it's hardly ever used. He's just Mr Lovejoy to all of us.

Originally, all the cooking you saw on the screen was prepared on the set while the programme was on the air. Our Prop Department used to put the ingredients together beforehand and whoever was supposed to be doing the cooking just got on with the job.

In one scene one of the characters, played by a Scot, was required to eat some porridge. He didn't approve of our efforts at all and afterwards he went round the studio complaining that what we had called porridge was an insult to any Scotsman. I'm Scottish, but I'm no porridge expert so I don't really know if he was justified in all this or not, but his remarks caused something of a furore at the time. Since then, we have had all the food precooked in our canteen by professional cooks.

Even so there have been many occasions when salt has been put in the sugar bowl. I like to think it was a mistake for I don't know if you've ever tasted salted tea but, believe me, it's simply dreadful.

We still make our own cups of tea and coffee and this resulted in Bill Avenell being quite ill one day. He had been given a cup of tea in the kitchen and the cup had previously been used for salad oil. The tea must have been atrocious but as this was a transmission, Bill carried on manfully sipping it. When the scene ended, he rushed out of the studio and was violently sick.

Bill is usually seen about the motel in traditional chef's uniform though in real life he knows nothing about haute cuisine. He's certainly no Escoffier.

'I hardly ever cook anything at home,' he admits. 'But I can carve a joint of lamb the right way and whenever there is a scene involving the kitchen staff, the scriptwriters make a point of having me on hand.

'Nowadays, of course, the head chef is more of an administrator, so I'm not required to cook anything personally.'

It is always real meat, eggs, and other ingredients you see on the set and when you see food being eaten it's the real thing.

Since eating is not usually a very attractive business to watch on the screen, actors and actresses have always been taught to take small mouthfuls of everything. Consequently quite a lot of tasty food remains uneaten ... by the cast at any rate. Though I'm sure quite a few of the studio staff are around to make sure nothing is wasted.

Food also gets taken home—to pets.

For kitchen scenes we'll spend £7 on a joint. Net sacks, which show the contents, are used for the sprouts, potatoes, and other vegetables. And it's always six or eight cabbages. Never just one—after all, this is an hotel kitchen and not a home.

The character of Mr Booth—who originally ran a Midlands employment and escort agency—was really developed by David Lawton, the actor who plays the part.

176

He came to read some scripts for us and was booked for four weeks. That was five years ago!

The part of Mr Booth was a straightforward characterization with which any competent actor could well cope. But David decided to turn him into, as he puts it, 'an amiable near-eccentric'.

He turned up in the studio for the dress rehearsal wearing spectacles and a bow tie. In real life he wears neither.

This straightaway seemed to establish Mr Booth as a somewhat prissy, precise gentleman—the type of man you might find serving in the exotic food department of a large West End store.

Reg Watson was delighted and, on the strength of David's interpretation, he had the role of Mr Booth greatly enlarged.

Some device had to be thought up to keep him permanently on the *Crossroads* scene so Mr Booth found himself engaged as a chef, after deputizing for a temporary chef who had failed to report for duty.

This, in turn, has led to some exhausting exchanges between Mr Lovejoy and Mr Booth.

'He takes himself too seriously,' says David. 'Mr Booth is always so earnest, so correct. He's a stickler for doing everything the right way and when things go wrong, as they inevitably do, then everyone has a lot of fun at Mr Booth's expense.'

David Lawton is also an accomplished playwright. One of his plays, a sophisticated comedy *I'll Sleep in the Spare Room* is being put on tour, prior to West End presentation.

After working with John Bentley on *Crossroads*, he suggested John for the lead in one of his radio plays *Who Was Norma Stone?* This resulted in John joining the BBC's Radio Repertory Company.

With this kind of background, it's not surprising that David takes a great interest not only in the characterization of the role of Mr Booth but also in the dialogue with which he is involved. It was David, in fact, who first added those immortal words, 'Don't worry, Mrs Richardson. Leave

177

everything to me ...', whenever he is about to embark on some project or task that we all know is doomed to failure.

They weren't in the script, but they've helped to establish Mr Booth's character and I always cap his remark with a wince—just to show you all that I know, perfectly, the outcome of his endeavours.

Mr Booth means well. But he always fails.

David has another catchline which he uses. Whenever he is due to leave the serial for a while his final words are always the same.

'If anyone wants me, I'll be in the storeroom.'

By using this device, we can bring him back into the plot whenever he is needed.

I have known poor Mr Booth to stay in that storeroom for as long as ten months.

David has been in several episodes of *Maigret, Z Cars, Vendetta*, and other top television series but this was his first encounter with a daily serial and his reaction was typical.

'I don't know how you do it,' he told me. 'It's such a tight schedule. Every other serial is on an output of two shows a week but *Crossroads* is twice as fast, first five shows a week and now four.

'On the other hand, this is one of the happiest studios I have ever worked in. You're all one happy family. How do you do it?'

I gave him the answer straight away.

'Because that's the only way *Crossroads* can happen. There's no time for temperament. No time for quarrels. We're working too hard. We have to be a happy family, otherwise there wouldn't be a *Crossroads*.'

But not all the viewers are happy with our efforts and we still get some odd complaints ...

One woman viewer sent a letter saying she could see the dark roots in the hair of two of the cast—Jane Rossington and Sue Hanson.

'I'm a blonde myself,' she wrote. 'But I always take trouble with my hair and they should do the same, especially as they're on television.'

In one episode we had Bruce Richardson (Michael Walker) telling Mrs Rigby (Nancy Gower) that the district nurse had offered to cook Edward Rigby's dinner.

This brought a swift protest from a number of district nurses who pointed out that no district nurse would undertake domestic work of this nature and that it would be the duty of a home help to prepare a meal in such circumstances —not a district nurse.

But we also manage to please the nursing profession from time to time.

One of our most devoted fans is Miss Eunice Vickery, assistant matron at an old people's home in Wimbledon, London.

Miss Vickery wrote to tell us that she had seen every episode ever screened in the London area. We decided she must be our Champion *Crossroads* viewer so we invited her to come to Birmingham to attend one of our studio parties and see how the show is put together before the cameras.

She is still enjoying our adventures and she wrote saying so when I won the *Sun* Television Award.

CHAPTER TWELVE

Love makes the world go round—or so they say. Certainly there have been plenty of love stories, thought up by the script team, among the various characters who come and go at Meg's motel.

We've had our real-life romances too—no less than five weddings and they blossomed without any help from anyone, except the couples themselves ...

Our first big romance started even before we came on the air. Tim Jones, one of our original directors who had started as a trainee and worked with me on *Lunch Box* and other ATV shows, met Jane Rossington when she turned up at our very first rehearsal to become my TV daughter.

After the first two days of working together, Tim offered Jane a lift in his car. This happened in October and, as the weeks of preparation went past, they saw more and more of each other so that the rest of us were very soon aware that we had a real-life romance in our midst.

The following May they were married. I was at the wedding and so was John Bentley. Tony Morton, who was playing Carlos the Spanish chef and can now be seen on the hoardings as a French monk advertising Normandy butter and cheese, was the best man.

As Jane's TV Mum I even found myself shedding a tear as she walked up the aisle. It was a strange feeling to see one's 'daughter', whom I had only known for six months, become a bride.

The wedding was a big event in the Midlands. The couple had photographs and headlines in the local Press and they were interviewed on our daily news magazine *ATV Today*. Love in real life had come to *Crossroads*.

But as with our *Crossroads* romances, not every marriage can be happy and successful. Things started to go wrong for Tim and Jane when, after directing more than two hundred and thirty editions of our serial, Tim decided he wanted a change and went off to work as a freelance director.

We had quite a party, for it was our first *Crossroads* departure. As well as giving him some farewell presents we also formed a choir and sang a special version of *Now is the Hour*, with appropriate up-dated lyrics. One of the lines went 'Now is the Hour for Tim to say Good-bye'.

He had been associated with us from the start and it was sad to see him leave. As far as I was concerned, I felt I was losing a son-in-law. After all, he *was* married to my daughter! As it turned out, my feeling was justified for his departure from our Birmingham studios meant he saw less and less of Jane.

They had only been married for just over two years and it was not without its irony that while Jane continued to work in *Crossroads*, her husband was directing episodes of ITV's rival serial *Coronation Street*.

They had a flat in Kew, West London, but as Tim had to work for Granada in Manchester and Jane had to work for ATV in Birmingham, they spent very little time together at their London home.

Finally the break came and after five years they decided to end their marriage. The eventual parting was a sorrowful occasion—not only for Jane but also for me as her TV mother.

The rest of the cast were well aware of what was happening and we determined to give Jane all the help and support we could. Reg Watson arranged for some special scenes to be included which would keep Jane busy and occupied—not only at rehearsals and before the cameras but also when she was alone at night learning her lines. There's nothing like hard work to take one's mind off one's troubles.

Jane did what the rest of us have had to do from time to time. She plunged into her career with a new strength and dedication.

'*Crossroads* saved me,' she admits. 'Work kept me going. I'm sure I would have had a nervous breakdown if there hadn't been the regular routine of the studios—the rehearsals, the hard work, and everything else that goes with working in a TV serial.'

Every day, Jane and the rest of us were involved in some drama or other on the screen—but none of the millions who watched us knew of the emotional drama of two young people's broken marriage that was going on behind the scenes.

We had all worked together; we had all been involved in the romance from the start; we had all been at the wedding and now our first romance was crumbling around us.

Jane naturally took it all very badly but somehow she managed to carry on. No wonder she has lost two stone in weight since *Crossroads* began!

As it happens, both she and Tim have now remarried and I am happy to tell you that everything is working out well for them both. Jane has married a businessman and they live at Sutton Coldfield; while Tim's wife is a dancer, Deidre Holton, and he works for Thames Television.

But it did seem odd that the actor playing Jane's TV husband, Edward Clayton, was actually best man at her real ex-husband's second marriage.

The world of television is very closely knit—and small. If such coincidences can happen away from the studios, then it is hardly surprising when our writers invent similar circumstances on the screen.

When Jane first joined us, she was supposed to be seventeen years old but her real age was twenty. Montague Lyon, who was then ATV's casting director in London, had used her as probationer nurse Kate Ford for two years in *Emergency–Ward 10* and he suggested Jane for the role of my daughter.

At that time Jane was in York Repertory Company playing in *Alfie*. She had a phone call to come down to see Reg Watson in Birmingham so as she was only in the first act, she slipped away without telling anyone and missed the final curtain so as to be in Birmingham first thing the following morning.

She read the part for Reg on a Wednesday.

'Fine,' he said. 'Can you start on Monday?'

So Jane went back to York and they agreed to release her. She came along to the studios on the Monday morning expecting, like the rest of us, that it was just six weeks' work.

No one thought beyond that ...

As my TV daughter, Jane has now been married three years but in real life she has been married for the second time for two years, so we were all very excited when she told us one morning that she was expecting her first baby.

'Good,' said Reg. 'We'll write it into the script that you are pregnant and you just carry on working. That is, if you want to.'

'Of course I want to,' Jane told him.

As it happened, Jane had a miscarriage and the idea of my becoming a grandmother had to be abandoned.

Some months later, Reg approached Jane and said he thought it was about time she *did* have a baby in *Crossroads*. He put it as tactfully as he could, under the circumstances, but Jane had now recovered from the unhappiness of losing her own baby and she readily agreed to become a make-believe mother on TV.

Three months later this development appeared in the script. Jane had to tell me that she was expecting a baby.

But the strange part about all this is that on the very day she was to tell me on the *Crossroads* set that she was pregnant she also told me she was pregnant again—in real life.

Our second *Crossroads* love story came when Pamela Greenall, an Australian actress from Melbourne, married Graham Weston, a Birmingham actor whose family are well-known Midlands jewellers.

In her *Crossroads* life, Pamela had been Meg's friend, Ruth Bailey, whose husband Gerald was killed by a hit-and-run driver. Then she married Meg's brother, Andy Fraser

(Ian Patterson), a fine Scottish actor who left us to resume his singing career.

Pamela joined us four months after we started. Reg Watson had seen her when she was working at the Alexandra Repertory and a few months later, when she was working at Leicester Repertory, she came over to be auditioned. As it happened, there was a mix-up over the scripts. Peter Harris, the floor manager, now a producer at our Elstree studios, gave her the wrong script—the part of a sixteen-year-old girl.

Pamela dutifully read it but Reg, in the control room watching her on the monitors, realized a mistake had been made and came down into the studio to put things right.

Adept at improvisation, being able to spread, to continue talking even though there were no words left in the script, Pamela had just the right background we needed for our TV repertory company. Once she and I had a whole sequence in which she did nothing but talk about Christmas cards—because the floor manager had signalled that extra time was needed.

Soon after Pamela joined us, a young twenty-year-old actor came for an audition. He had been at the Birmingham Theatre School and his first job had been at the Alhambra, Bradford, in a play by Walter Greenwood which he had specially written for some of the *Coronation Street* characters, in the hope that it would be a hit.

The play folded and Graham Weston came to us. It was only our second week and he appeared in Episodes 2 and 3 playing a thug in a café.

The following February he returned for a longer spell in the role of Ken Church, a taxi driver. He knew several of the cast, particularly David Fennell who had been at drama school with him.

'Who's the bird in trousers?' Graham asked his friend.

David introduced him to Pamela and this is how they got to know each other. Graham was then only just starting his acting career; he was not very sure of himself and hadn't very much money. *Crossroads* was his first job on television.

184

A few weeks later, Pamela said to him at rehearsals, 'It's my birthday today. Like to join me for lunch at the Albany? It's my treat.'

The two went off together and this was the start of their romance.

While Graham was in *Crossroads*, BBC producer Anthony Cornish spotted him and secured him for the BBC's twice-weekly serial *United* in which he appeared for fifteen months.

This meant he could see a great deal more of Pamela and they actually did their courting while she was in *Crossroads* for ATV and Graham was working round the corner for the BBC in *United*.

Graham found working for the BBC a lot easier than working for us. In one week the *United* cast were only expected to produce fifty minutes' programming—less than an hour.

But one week with *Crossroads* meant two hours of air time.

Graham is now an established actor. He and Pamela live in Warwickshire with their four-year-old daughter, and he is seen in many of the current TV series and serials such as *Z Cars, Softly, Softly, The Persuaders*.

Last year he was filming the comedy *Percy's Progress* in which he plays Cpl Brian Harris.

Crossroads not only launched him as an actor, but found him a bride as well.

The next *Crossroads* couple to marry were singer Deke Arlon, who played Benny Wilmot, a pop singer, and Gillian Betts who was Josefina, wife of Carlo, the chef.

As Josefina, Gillian—one of our early regulars—stayed with us for our first Christmas at *Crossroads* on a supposed visit to England. But she seemed so very much at home, that she was re-booked to return at Easter and Gillian remained with us for seven years.

Josefina spent much of her time in the kitchen getting her feet wet. Although we had water on tap, there was no plumbing to take it away, just a bucket beneath the sink. If the bucket—out of camera vision of course—happened to be badly positioned, or someone forgot to empty it, then whoever was at the kitchen sink would get their feet flooded with the overflowing water.

Such minor catastrophies always seem to happen during actual transmissions—never at rehearsals.

Gillian came to us during a year's lectureship at a Birmingham technical college, where she was teaching English and Drama. This meant that after working as an actress during the daytime, she had to rush to the other side of Birmingham to take her classes at night.

As she couldn't always fit them in, she took some of her pupils in private tutorship at her parents' home in Sutton Coldfield.

I hoped she used her experience as a practical illustration of how tough life in the acting profession can sometimes be.

Deke and Gillian live in a £70,000 house in Buckinghamshire with their two boys, James, four, and Timothy, two.

Deke is now managing director of York Records and Chevron Music, subsidiaries of Trident TV. Singers with whom he is associated include Gilbert O'Sullivan, James Taylor, Kenny Young, and The Sweet. The last time I saw him he had chalked up twenty-two hits and been involved in the sale of 17,000,000 records.

'I owe it all to *Crossroads*,' declares Deke. 'This is the show that gave me my start and this is what established me. It's a wonderful show and Reg Watson is a wonderful person.'

So it's not only performers that *Crossroads* has helped— but recording executives too.

Deke's association with Reg goes back to the days when he was appearing for him in an ATV pop show *For Teenagers Only*. Later, Deke brought out a record for EMI *I'm Just a Boy* and Reg booked him to sing the song to Marilyn (then played by Sue Nichols) in one episode of *Crossroads*.

Some dialogue had to be worked out for Deke to say but when it came to him saying it he just dried up. He could sing well enough but he couldn't speak lines, so the scene had to be scrapped.

Some while later, Deke rang up Reg and asked if he could have a regular part on *Crossroads*.

'But you can't say lines,' Reg told him.

'Give me another chance,' pleaded Deke.

So Reg agreed to audition him. Meanwhile Deke went around reading books, articles, anything in print—just to get used to speaking dialogue and remembering lines.

A sample scene was sent to him to learn. In the situation he was supposed to be an Italian salesman trying to sell a transistor radio.

Deke duly arrived in Birmingham to be auditioned and Margaret French took the part of Josefina, to whom he was supposed to be selling the radio. The dialogue went something like this:

Margaret: 'It's very nice looking.'

But not a word came from Deke—just a sigh.

Margaret: 'You think it has a good tone?'

Again no words. Only an enormous sigh.

Margaret, puzzled, looked at him and said the line again.

Another great sigh. Nothing more.

This was all too much for Reg Watson.

'I thought you said you could read lines,' he said. 'What's this strange noise you're making?'

'I'm sighing,' replied Deke.

'You're what?'

'Sighing—see it says so in the script "*Si*".'

'Deke,' said Reg, 'that's not a sigh. You are supposed to say it—"*Si*" is Italian for "Yes".'

At the end of all this Deke *did* get the job and was with us for three years.

He was only meant to stay a few weeks but the viewers wrote in and liked him so much he stayed longer and became Marilyn's boyfriend.

During one of his breaks from the programme he went on a series of one-night stands, as a singer, in Ulster, solely on the strength of his TV role.

Northern Ireland audiences have always like our programme and it is always high in the ratings there, so the
personal appearance of Benny Willmot was such a box-
office attraction that although he was only booked for a
five days' tour, he stayed for a year and made quite a lot of
money.

Reg Watson and I went over and I made some personal
appearances with Deke. We were both delighted that *Crossroads* had been responsible for his big success there.

At the end of the year he returned to the programme and
it was then that he fell in love with Gillian Betts and they
became engaged. But as they were both acting, they found
it impossible to persuade any mortgage company to lend
them money for a house so Deke decided on a career else-
where and quit the show.

He started with a record company at £19·50 a week, much
less than he was getting with us. Deke worked for six years
as an office boy learning the record business—and also to
get that mortgage.

When he and Gillian had saved enough, they got married
and Norman Jones, a National Theatre actor who had been
Ralph, the *Crossroads* milkman, was best man. Norman is
now godfather to their children; Alex Marshall (Christine,
the waitress who married Ralph) is their godmother. Alex,
incidentally, is completing a directors' training course with
Granada TV.

The Arlons are happy and established ... thanks to
Crossroads. At their home they have three gold albums;
nine gold singles, and five silver discs to celebrate the hit
records that Deke has produced.

Not bad for a *Crossroads* singer!

Another studio wedding came when Diane Keen married
Paul Greenwood.

Diane, twenty-seven, who played the haughty young
Empress Elizabeth of Austria from fifteen to twenty-six in
the BBC's £500,000 production of *Fall of Eagles* (Margaret
Leighton played her as an older woman), was with us for a
long time.

She played a very different role to that of an Empress. She was Sandra Gould, a cockney waitress with a crush on Paul Stevens, our motel manager. From downstairs with *Crossroads* to upstairs with *Fall of Eagles*.

Paul Greenwood, thirty, had the role of the manager and it wasn't long before Diane and Paul were attracted to each other, not only as *Crossroads* characters, but in real life too. They became engaged during the show and soon after leaving us they were married.

Diane, who had been with the Bristol Old Vic, was originally given the role of Sandra for three months but she did so well that she stayed for thirteen. The couple met at rehearsals and as the story line developed, they found things becoming more and more difficult as they went along.

'You see, in our TV characters we were supposed to be fond of each other and not show it,' says Paul. 'This meant every time we had a scene together in front of the camera, we were playing directly opposite to our real feelings.'

Paul's role as a trainee-manager lasted nine months, then he went off to appear as Aladdin in a Windsor pantomime. To explain his absence from the screen, we pretended he had gone on a trainee catering course.

When he returned to the motel he found promotion awaiting him—he took over the managership and stayed another three months.

But finally Paul left for other engagements and we explained his departure by saying he had gone to take over an hotel in Guernsey. Diane wanted to leave as well, so our scriptwriters arranged for Sandra to go to Guernsey on holiday and to like it so much that she decided to stay.

From time to time, Meg gets letters saying how happy they are together for they married in *Crossroads* just as they have married in real life.

BBC viewers saw Paul in Lulu's last TV series—he played in all the sketches with her. He has also done a *Comedy Playhouse* for the BBC.

Diane had several amusing scenes in the kitchen when she was Sandra Gould—especially when that coffee machine

189

of ours didn't work. However, she would always rise to the occasion and put in an off-the-cuff remark to cover things up.

Instead of saying something like, 'Isn't the coffee good today?' she would substitute, 'I'm sorry, you can't have any coffee today—the machine isn't working again.'

Diane used to visit her parents sometimes and drive herself back to the studios from London. One morning she rang Reg, just before we were about to tape the first programme, to say she had been involved in an accident with a lorry.

'I'm all right—just a few cuts and bruises,' she explained. 'But the car's a wreck. I'll try to get a lift and be with you as soon as I can.'

This time it was Roger's turn to speak Diane's lines, for we still had to go ahead with the recording. The dialogue that was written for the two of them had to be changed into a monologue for Roger—to keep the story going and ensure that viewers understood what was happening in the current plot.

Roger managed it all very smoothly and everything passed off as though nothing was wrong.

When it came to the afternoon recording, Diane had arrived in the studio after hitching a lift from a friendly lorry driver who turned out to be such a fan of *Crossroads* he drove her right up to the studio door.

Sue Hanson, who plays Diane Lawton, is the latest young actress to find a husband in *Crossroads*. Earlier this year she married Carl Wayne, the singer, in a spring wedding.

The couple met in the Rum Runner restaurant in Broad Street, Birmingham, when Sue looked in there with a girl-friend, after rehearsals, so they already knew each other when he joined us as Colin, the milkman.

On the first occasion that Carl was playing this role, he was delivering some milk and put the crate down with such force on the reception desk he spilt milk all over Joy Andrews (Mrs Hope).

It's Carl you hear singing the *New Faces* theme song

You're a Star, ATV's Saturday night talent show on which I sometimes appear as a panellist to judge the talent.

Sue got her job in *Crossroads* as a teenager when she was actually flat broke. Trained at the Webber Douglas Drama School, she had been with Bristol Old Vic for a year and was looking for a job when her agent fixed for her to have an audition for *Crossroads*.

She hitch-hiked on a lorry to Birmingham, auditioned for Reg Watson, and then had to hitch-hike back to London. Although ATV pay fares for auditions, the money takes about two weeks to arrive. By the time Sue reached home, the phone was ringing. It was her agent to tell her she had landed the role.

Sue has been with us for over eight years, although the original plan was for her to appear for eight weeks. The role of Diane was developed into that of an unmarried mother, *Crossroads* first real scandal. The father is Frank Adam, a film star, but he doesn't accept responsibility for fear of damaging his public image.

The Independent Television Authority, as it then was, did not censor the scandal itself but they wouldn't allow us to use the phrase 'unmarried mother'.

They ordered the words to be deleted from the script. Instead, we were told we could only make reference to her 'illegitimate baby'.

Here again there were difficulties. The child was supposed to be a boy but the first baby we used was in fact a girl. As the story progressed, the baby not only grew bigger too soon but it *looked* a girl too, instead of a boy.

The second child we used presented an even greater headache. Every time Sue held him he burst into tears. It happened at rehearsals. It happened on transmission. I have never heard a baby cry so much.

But on the other hand, this extra touch of realism seemed to fit in well with the story so we all carried on regardless.

In the story line, of course, Sue gets married to Vince Parker, the postman (Peter Brookes). This marriage doesn't work out too well and poor Sue finishes up an alcoholic.

For six months, every time she was in front of the camera, she had to give the impression of being affected by drink—but not exactly reeling drunk, just glazed and a little unsteady.

One day I asked her how she managed this.

'I do it by *thinking* drunk,' she explained. 'If you *think* you're sloshed you behave as though you are. It isn't difficult.'

I'm not so sure. Fortunately Meg hasn't turned to drink yet. If she does, I'll know what to do.

Everyone agreed that Sue made a great job of her role as an alcoholic, though in real life she drinks very little. One of the main reasons for her success is that once again, we sought advice from experts.

As well as our medical advisers assisting here, we also consulted the Birmingham Council on Alcoholism and they gave us advice based on their own case histories. This is why we were able to deal so accurately both in Sue's dialogue and behaviour.

The whole subject was researched most carefully. We also had a phone call from a self-confessed alcoholic after Sue started drinking heavily, on the screen.

He told us her portrayal was very lifelike and he even came to our studios to check the scripts for us.

Another viewer called later from Bristol—a woman this time—to tell us she had, for the first time, seen herself as she really was by watching Sue on the screen.

She rang to thank us and said she would be visiting Alcoholics Anonymous the following day.

And this of course was the whole purpose of that particular story line—to show the dangers of heavy drinking and how alcoholics could be helped—and cured.

But no one minds a glass or two of champagne to celebrate a wedding ... and this is how Sue and Carl celebrated last March when they were married at the Birmingham Registry Office. They wanted a quiet wedding so there was no announcement and no arrangements were made beforehand. We all knew about the wedding in *Crossroads* but we agreed not to tell anyone the time or place, for that's what Sue wanted.

Our fifth *Crossroads* bride chose an Italian silk knitted top with matching skirt for her bridal gown and they had tickets booked for a Rome honeymoon.

However on the day before the wedding, Carl was appearing as a guest singer on *The Golden Shot*. Charlie Williams who was then the compere, presented him with a silver tea set on the show and congratulated him on his wedding the next day.

Golden Shot goes out as a live transmission and the presentation and Charlie's announcement of a Birmingham wedding the following morning came as a complete surprise to Carl. The result of course was that when they arrived at the Registry Office they found themselves facing a whole crowd of *Crossroads* fans—about a thousand of them, plus pressmen and photographers.

Sue and Carl had to fight their way through. They were almost mobbed. Their quiet wedding was nearly a riot.

Crossroads may have tried to keep Sue's wedding out of the picture—but *Golden Shot* scored a bull's-eye.

CHAPTER THIRTEEN

Bearded Edward Clayton, thirty-four, might never have become my TV son-in-law, Stan Harvey, if he hadn't had an accident on his motor cycle.

At that time he was in repertory at Stoke-on-Trent and had been involved in a crash with a police car. His machine was a write-off. He only had third-party insurance and his hire-purchase debt.

Edward had been trained at the same drama school in Sidcup, Kent, as Jane Rossington and when Jane heard we were looking for someone to play her husband she suggested her fellow student.

Edward didn't hesitate. He asked Stoke Repertory to release him from his contract—which had another five months to run—they agreed and he was soon able to pay off his hire-purchase debt.

Edward, who lives in a Staffordshire farmhouse and has two girls and a boy, has also been seen in *Coronation Street, Z Cars,* and other TV programmes—usually playing a policeman.

Under the name of Tommy Rushton, he has also written two of our story lines which ran for a couple of months. In one of them, Stan and his father Wilf (Morris Parsons) revisited their old home at Cradley Heath, in the Black Country, and in the other situation there was a problem over Stan's actual parentage—as to whether he is really Wilf's son, or not.

Before Stan married Jill she was married to John Crane, then managing the motel. Crane turned out to be a bigamist and he left.

Stan comes from a typical working-class family—his Dad

is a pigeon fancier—while Jill has more of a middle-class background.

The fact that Jill now seems to have married somewhat beneath her, has not escaped the notice of many of our *Crossroads* fans. Edward is always showing me letters he keeps receiving from Jill's many fans—criticizing him for marrying Meg Richardson's daughter.

This shows how right Jane Rossington was in suggesting Edward for the part—she obviously knew he would make a great job of it. As I've often told him, 'If they take you for real, then you've succeeded.'

'Quite a few people seem to think Jill should be married to a real smoothie,' says Edward. 'They seem to forget that when she *was* married to one of those smooth-speaking gents he turned out a complete rotter who did the dirty on her.

'I play Stan Harvey for what he's supposed to be—an ordinary working-class sort of chap.

'But I know a lot of viewers resent my TV image. I get letters telling me I need a shave or that I should have a haircut. There are even two eighteen-year-old Brighton girls who are always writing to tell me to get lost and that I'm not good enough to be Meg Richardson's son-in-law.

'In their latest letters they say they are now switching off every time I come on the screen. If this is so, they must be missing quite a lot of *Crossroads*, as I am often on the screen continuously for weeks.

'These two girls have never given their full addresses so I have never been able to write to them. Maybe it's just as well, for Stan Harvey really is most unpopular with them. They just hate his guts.'

This kind of reaction from viewers used to upset Edward. But he has been with us now for over three years so, like the rest of us, he just has to put up with it.

Unlike the BBC, ITV has an agreement with Equity over the employment of non-professionals.

This means that no one can appear on ITV unless he or she is a member of the actors' trade union.

Equity will, however, accept a performer in membership if they can show they have made six appearance in television programmes.

So when our casting department is approached by extras for parts in *Crossroads* they have to be turned down if they cannot produce an Equity card. But if they come back with Equity membership after working for the BBC, then they can appear in *Crossroads*.

We have had a number of good performers over the years who have come to us on this basis.

One of them is Anthony Waters, whose father is a wholesale fish merchant in Birmingham. Anthony had appeared in a number of amateur productions in the Midlands as an actor and singer and he was very keen to get into our serial.

Upon learning about the Equity situation, he approached the BBC and they gave him some walk-on parts at £11 a time in such programmes as *Lord Peter Wimsey*, *The Brothers*, and *Owen MD* which were taped at their new Pebble Mill studios in Birmingham.

After six months he had his Equity card and his first job at the motel was to go up to the bar and buy a drink.

Now that he was acceptable to ITV, he wrote in for an audition on *New Faces*, ATV's Saturday night talent show. At that time he was also appearing in an amateur production of *Camelot* as King Arthur.

When it came his turn to audition, he walked on the stage and surprised everyone, including Les Cocks the producer, by appearing in his full King Arthur regalia.

He was booked for *New Faces* and was a winning finalist. On the strength of this, Alan Blackburn, the agent, offered him a summer season at Blackpool but Anthony chose to stay in the Midlands.

Since then, he has auditioned for a speaking role in *Crossroads* and is now Bill Miller, a friend of Hugh Mortimer who came to see me at the motel with some papers from Australia.

196

Another young actor who has managed to change the original image devised for him in *Crossroads* is Johnny Briggs who plays Clifford Layton, the former prisoner who came to work in the motel and then was recognized by Mr Booth, a prison visitor, as someone he had seen inside jail serving a sentence.

Layton then left our employment but consequently won several thousands of pounds playing poker and he is now back running a reciprocal travel deal in which guests at *Crossroads* can have car hire facilities available for them, plus other amenities, at an hotel in Italy.

The part of Clifford Layton was that of a somewhat unscrupulous, unlikeable character but Johnny has managed to stamp something of his own personality on the part and infect the role with such charm that he has now become a rather lovable scoundrel.

On top of all this, he has been falling in love with Diane and, although she doesn't want anything to do with him at the moment, there is always the chance she may relent.

Johnny used to be on the other side of the law—as Det. Sgt Ruffel in *No Hiding Place* with Raymond Francis. He is also in a new comedy series for LWT *Thick as Thieves* but here, as with *Crossroads*, he is again something of a rogue.

During all the years I have been with *Crossroads* I cannot recall ever having actually forgotten my lines— except with Johnny Briggs.

It happened when he was explaining to me, in the character of Clifford Layton, how he had arranged for this Italian hotel to have self-drive cars awaiting *Crossroads* guests on their arrival at Rome airport.

It was quite a long, intricate speech. I was listening attentively and he made such a good job of it all that I found myself quite absorbed. When he had finished, he kept looking at me and I kept looking at him—nodding for him to carry on.

When no words came I suddenly realized that he was

waiting for me to speak—so I covered up as best I could. When the transmission was over, Johnny came up to me and said, 'What happened? You "went".'

'Gracious,' I said. 'Was it me? I thought it was you. That's the first time it's ever happened to me.'

And we both had a good laugh.

I must explain that in television terms, when performers forget their lines or dry up we use the expression that they 'went'.

I don't know how it originated—probably it means that we go off somewhere in our minds, outer space or something like that.

Anyway this was an occasion when I 'went'. Believe me, it can happen to anyone.

It was quite a thrill for us all when Derek Farr arrived at the studios to play the part of the penurious Timothy Hunter, David Hunter's uncle.

Reg Watson had persuaded Derek to join us and it was his first experience of working flat out on a TV serial. All in all, he has appeared in forty-five episodes. But of course he came to us with a tremendous background of films in which he had starred—more than thirty.

Derek had been one of my heroes for years, after seeing him as leading man in many stage and screen hits. But this was the first time we had worked together and he found television very different to film making—particularly our kind of television.

'It's the speed at which you all work that is so astonishing,' he told me. 'You get through about eighty minutes of television a week. When I was in a film studio we'd be lucky to get two minutes a day in the can and as there was a lot of wastage, those two minutes might well finish up on the cutting-room floor. This never happens with *Crossroads*.'

After a lifetime in films, Derek, at sixty-two, has made a new career for himself in television as a character actor although, he tells me, he still finds TV producers tend to think of him solely in terms of film roles which, after all, pay very much more money than television.

'The TV people seem to think I wouldn't be interested in appearing for them but of course I am,' he says. 'This is why I was very pleased when Reg offered me the part of Timothy Hunter.

'The only TV serial in which I had appeared was *Coronation Street*—a single appearance as the managing director of a brewery.

'The atmosphere in *Coronation Street* was very different. All the time I was there, none of the regular cast ever spoke to me. I used to say "Good morning" to them but they didn't even answer.

'With *Crossroads* it was quite the opposite. You all made me welcome from the start and it's been that way ever since. I'm rather a shy sort of chap and I was a bundle of nerves when I first arrived on the set, but within a few minutes you had made me feel one of the family.

'It was such a relief after the way I had been treated at *Coronation Street*. You've no idea the difference it made.'

Derek also made a few suggestions to Reg Watson about his portrayal of his role. Reg never minded listening to other people's ideas—sometimes he took their advice, other times he would disagree. In which case, the character remained as it was or the particular line of dialogue stayed unchanged.

In Derek Farr's case, Reg approved and Derek was able to give the role of Timothy Hunter a great deal of charm which might well have been lacking if the role had been played by someone else.

'I know he's a bit of a bounder but at least I'm trying to make him fairly likeable,' Derek explained.

Derek was very amused at our phone trick—something he hadn't encountered before. This is when the studio manager waves his arms and points to the telephone. The phone rings and whoever is nearest has to pick up the receiver and carry on an imaginary conversation with someone at the other end.

I have become quite an expert at this, over the years. You

may have seen me at work—carrying on a quite lengthy conversation at the end of some particular scene or other.

The reason for this is simple—extra material is needed to keep the scene, and the cameras, running. These situations are unique to a television serial like ours. They would never happen during film making or, indeed, in the taping of a television play.

But in a serial, because of the pace at which we work, it can often happen that we find ourselves reaching the end of a scene and running out of dialogue too soon.

Each *Crossroads* episode has to fill a certain fixed amount of air time and this is why we use the phone trick to keep going.

On one occasion, Derek happened to be nearest the phone when he received the studio manager's signal, relayed by the director in the control box, that we were running short.

Realizing what had happened, Derek waited for the phone to ring, picked it up, and invented a completely one-sided telephone conversation to fill in the extra time.

Jacqueline Stanbury, twenty-five, came to us direct from Oldham Repertory, after training with the Bristol Old Vic, for her first TV appearance.

She was Joanne Petersen, a friend of Meg's son Sandy. She was supposed to be visiting England after winning a *Funny Bone* competition in Canada and had to go around doing crazy things like cutting off men's ties, or similar japes, to try to make people laugh.

Jacqueline did very well with us and we wanted her to stay as a regular but she did agree to come back for a month later as Meg's secretary. On this occasion she was supposed to be looking after her sister's baby and this led to many complications as no one in the motel, except Sandy, knew she had the child with her.

The first week of the recording went fine. We had a real baby and it behaved splendidly. No cries and no tantrums. This was quite a relief all round. Then the second week just before transmission, someone remarked that the baby

200

looked a little strange. A closer look—and there was no doubt at all.

Our baby had chicken pox.

Alan Coleman, who was directing this particular episode, had to rush around to find another baby. He managed to borrow one, belonging to one of the secretaries, and we substituted the second baby for the first—just in time. As it happened, both children looked very much alike and no one spotted the baby switch.

Jacqueline is now an established television performer. She has been in comedy shows with Frankie Howerd and Dick Emery, played the leading role in one of the Granada plays *Seasons of the Year* with Dinah Sheridan and Thora Hird, and was in one of the BBC's *Play for Today* series *The Reporters*.

Her latest role—Policewoman Sally Hopkins in the BBC's long running *Dixon of Dock Green*.

Lynette Erving, twenty-seven, is another repertory actress who has been appearing with us—in the role of Pat McKenzie, working in the local post office.

Pat fell in love with postman Don Rogers (Albert Shepherd) and after some cliff-hanging suspense they eventually married.

Lynette learned her stage craft at a London drama school and has been in a number of TV productions including *Pardon My Genii* (Thames), *The Rivals of Sherlock Holmes* (Thames), and *Coronation Street* (Granada).

It was while she was appearing at the Alexandra Repertory Company in Birmingham for Derek Salberg that our casting director, Margaret French, booked her for *Crossroads*.

In fact she finished at the Alexandra Rep on the Saturday and started with us the following Monday. Lynette, married to a drama teacher and director, lives in Walthamstow and when she works on *Crossroads* stays overnight at the Birmingham YWCA.

As one of the few *Crossroads* performers to have also

worked in *Coronation Street* she is especially qualified to compare the two serials.

'I think the main difference is that *Coronation Street*, since it goes out only twice a week, is a much more leisurely business,' says Lynette. 'They all have twice the time and this is obviously an advantage.

'On the other hand, *Crossroads* succeeds because of the great teamwork behind it all. Everyone tries their utmost. It may have more rough edges than *Coronation Street* but the overall effect is usually much greater and it always seems to me much closer to life than its northern counterpart.'

Lynette also feels that a serial such as ours is much more interesting for an actress than the normal straight play of an hour's duration.

'You are given a character and then, in just an hour, you have to register all its emotions and feelings. This just isn't true to life. You can never get to know anyone in an hour.

'This is why a serial is much more realistic for an actress. You get the chance to develop the character. Everything happens much more slowly. You can play it as it really is— at life pace.'

Lynette travels up to Birmingham by train and you can imagine her anxiety when her Inter-City express was once stopped just north of St Albans because of a warning that a bomb was hidden in the baggage.

All the passengers had to alight. The train was searched and Lynette had visions of missing the vital dress rehearsal and recording session at our Birmingham studios.

However all was well.

When she arrived at our studios she found a similar bomb scare ...

Crossroads had been evacuated as well.

Nicola Rowley is another *Crossroads* girl. She was one of the leading ladies in Paul Raymond's *Pyjama Tops* at the Whitehall Theatre in London and has also been seen in such TV series as *Jason King* with Peter Wyngarde.

Maxine Cassin started with us. Since then she has gone on to many appearances on TV in *Doctor at Large, Man at the Top*, and *The Persuaders* with Tony Curtis and Roger Moore.

Performers come and go in *Crossroads*. They stay to take part in certain plot developments and then they leave. Sometimes performers would like-to stay longer but if viewers saw too many of the same faces they would become bored and their interest would flag.

It is always a sad moment when an artist gets written out of the series but most accept their departure gracefully and set about finding themselves another job.

An exception was Anthony Morton who had a long run with us as Carlos, the Spanish chef. Tony appeared in seven hundred and fifty episodes and when the time came for him to leave he was removed by the simple, if dramatic, trick of being killed off. Josefina, his Spanish wife, received a letter from Spain telling her she was a widow.

The heartbroken woman even had to attend a Mass for her late husband on Good Friday.

This was all too much for Tony who first learned of his death when he was watching the programme some weeks after he had left us.

He sent Reg Watson a black-edged mourning card, decorated with a sheaf of lilies in one corner.

On the face of the card Tony had written just four words: 'Wish You Were Here.'

But we had many laughs while Tony was with us. In one kitchen scene he was supposed to throw a saucepan at Sandy—and miss. But on transmission, by mistake the saucepan caught Sandy in the back of the neck and sent him sprawling.

Carlos always used to wear a chef's hat. He would take it off and put it beside him in the kitchen. It then became a habit for everyone to give it a karate chop as they went past. This used to annoy Tony as it knocked his chef's hat out of shape.

So to get even he put a heavy stage weight inside the hat and several of the cast went around with bruised hands for days.

Before leaving us, Tony had to fight a bull for a *Crossroads* story.

A relative in Spain had sent Carlos a matador's outfit and he had taken some bets with villagers that he would be able to master any bull they liked to produce.

Carlos was to lose his bet by being chased by the bull and jumping over a hedge to safety.

In our story, the bull came from Les Blundell, a local farmer whose wife Vi works at the motel. In real life it was being supplied by the Shropshire Farm Institute, near Shrewsbury.

Prior to the filming, director Alan Coleman had been over to arrange everything and the officials had shown him a very vicious animal in his pen, pawing the ground, snorting, and thumping away in true bull-ring style.

When Tony Morton arrived, Alan showed him the bull and told him this was the animal they had picked for the bullfight. Tony took it all in his stride. 'A magnificent creature,' he said, between the snorts. 'But I'd never get my cloak over its back and that would spoil the whole effect.'

Finally the Institute produced the bull that had been selected the previous evening. He was a fine animal but there was just one snag. He belonged to a particular breed which does not have horns. And a bull without horns didn't seem exactly right for our gallant bullfighter.

To cope with this, Alan had brought with him some papier mâché horns supplied by our Props Department, but when these were put on to the bull's head they kept falling down over his eyes whenever he moved.

At this point, the principal of the Institute suggested that we use a bull belonging to a farmer just along the lane.

'It will be just right for what you want,' he said. 'It'll chase anything that moves—but you'll have to move fast.'

So the bull was brought into the field in a horse-box. Tony

was sewn into his matador's outfit and the camera team were warned to film everything just as it happened.

'This bull moves like lightning,' said the farmer. 'You won't get a second chance.'

At a given signal the horse-box was opened and the bull was led out on a long lead by two farm hands. Tony Morton stood in the centre of the field waiting to dash to the hedge, with the bull in hot pursuit, and then leap to safety the other side.

But the bull came out of the box, looked at Tony—and just stood still. He didn't move.

'Run,' we called out to Tony.

Tony ran. But the bull just yawned.

'What do I do now?' called Tony.

'Perhaps he can't see you properly,' answered the director. 'Come a little closer.'

So Carlos the matador walked slowly up to the bull and stood there looking him straight in the face. Again no reaction. Then suddenly, the bull took off—but instead of chasing Tony it ran off in the opposite direction and Tony had to chase the bull.

Tony's pursuit ended at the edge of the field where the bull suddenly stopped and started chatting up a herd of cows.

He got quite excited over them too—snorting, eyes blazing, and providing just the reaction we wanted.

The cameras dutifully recorded everything and later we had Tony run across the field and jump over the hedge just as though the animal really had been in hot pursuit at his heels.

Thanks to some clever editing of the material, when the sequence reached the screen it really did look as though Tony had been chased by the bull. No one could tell it had been the other way round—with Tony chasing the bull.

Alan Coleman, who filmed this incident, was one of our original *Crossroads* directors and has now joined Reg Watson in Australia.

Alan began with ATV as a cameraman and after becoming a director, worked on *Crossroads* for seven and a half years before being promoted to a producer.

He was in charge of our successful children's drama series *The Kids From 47a*. He has joined the same organization as Reg—Reg Grundy Enterprises which supplies forty hours of television production a week to the Australian TV networks.

Reg has gone there to be Head of Drama and Alan is Head of Children's Drama.

The two of them worked very closely on *Crossroads*. Alan says that Reg is the only man he knows who has a 'twenty-four hours' brain—one that can think up ideas at one o'clock in the morning.'

In his early days as a *Crossroads* director, Alan was filming at a Midlands motel, seeking various sequences that could be inserted into our programme to provide added realism.

Our unit was working in the grounds of this particular establishment by arrangement with the management. Several blue ATV vans and trucks were parked around the premises when a smartly dressed, middle-aged man drove up to the reception area in a Jaguar, went in to sign the register, and then came out to drive off to one of the chalets.

His companion was a young, attractive blonde, in a mink coat.

Seeing their arrival, Alan told his camera team to film the couple and the whole scene was faithfully recorded. A few minutes later he was back in the motel when he was called to the phone.

'You don't know me and you never will,' said a man's voice. 'But if you use that film you've just taken I will sue you for every penny you've got.'

He was, of course, perfectly within his rights. Apart from not wanting anyone to know of his stay at the motel with a girlfriend, he also had the right not to appear on television in a drama production if he didn't wish to do so.

From a legal viewpoint, no one can be included in any TV drama programme without their permission, though this doesn't apply to news coverage.

Crossroads kept his secret.

CHAPTER FOURTEEN

Coincidences seem to haunt *Crossroads*.

There have been so many of them. To recall a few:

We had a scene in which a bomb was supposed to have arrived at the motel, in a parcel—but the ticking inside turned out to be an alarm clock.

The day after this was screened, the Midlands Press reported a similar incident in Wolverhampton. Their bomb also turned out to be an alarm clock.

We blew up part of the motel with an old wartime bomb that had lain undiscovered for years. This was in order to introduce a newly designed kitchen and give a face lift to several other rooms.

The following day there was a similar explosion in a motel in the USA. Their kitchen was also destroyed.

Vikki Chambers, a young Midlands actress, was thrown from her horse for one sequence and was supposed to have broken her neck—and survived.

A few weeks later she phoned Alan Coleman, who had directed this particular episode, to say that she had been thrown from her horse while out riding, had broken her neck, and was speaking to him while wearing a plaster cast.

We once had a phone call from Reg Watson telling us to cut the last three minutes from the script—just before we were due to go into the studio to record this particular episode.

The reason for this was that our story line involved the payment of key money for a flat and, at that particular moment, there was a similar row going on in Birmingham involving the payment of such money to some property company.

Crossroads couldn't get involved by having the same situation on the screen and so we had to cut out our ending.

Tim Jones, who was directing, came to me and explained what had happened.

'I'll write you a new scene,' he said. And off he went to do it.

He was soon back with the extra material. There just wasn't time to involve any other members of the cast, getting them to learn lines, rehearse and so on, so we used the customary trick of having Meg Richardson make a phone call.

Tim gave me three minutes of monologue to learn—it had something to do with my trying to explain to a Pakistani plumber that I wanted some new pipes fitted—and he used this for the end of the episode instead of the scene we had rehearsed.

These last-minute complications and difficulties happen all the time with a long-running serial like ours.

I remember one occasion when John Bentley was stricken with flu while in his Birmingham digs. He was due to record a scene in which he was appearing with a number of children.

This particular sequence was an integral part of the story and it was quite impossible to scrap it without the collapse of the whole format of *Crossroads* at that particular moment.

Reg Watson came up with the solution. He arranged for a recording unit to visit John at his sick bed. Then with John lying in bed, the sound technicians recorded his dialogue—leaving gaps in between.

Back in the studio, Reg had hired an extra who, as near as possible, had the same build as John Bentley *when seen from behind*. This actor then sat with his back to the camera with the children, whom he was supposed to be questioning, facing him.

As far as the viewers were concerned they *thought* they were seeing Bentley's back. They certainly *heard* Bentley's voice because we used the sound track made at his bedside.

The children's answers were fitted into the gaps left in the original bedside recording.

Don Maclean, the Birmingham comic who was a big success in variety at the London Palladium and who is the host of *Crackerjack* for BBC television, started his TV career with us—as a member of the pop group that Benny Wilmot had.

Their stage name was Georgie Saint and the Dragons and Don was one of the Dragons.

Don was at the same drama school in Birmingham as David Fennell and where Roger Tonge had half a dozen lessons, and might well have stayed an actor but for one reason—money.

After appearing with us he was offered two jobs—one as assistant stage manager in a repertory company producing *Anthony and Cleopatra* for £6.50 a week; the other, as second comic for a summer season at Skegness—for £18 a week.

Don took the Skegness job and has stayed a stand-up variety comedian ever since. He had a six months' season with the Black and White Minstrels at London's Victoria Palace and, last summer, was with them at Paignton, Devon. He has made a number of guest appearances on all the top television shows, both for the BBC and ITV.

While he was with us a quite dramatic incident occurred which passed off as a joke. Carolyn Lyster left the *Crossroads* lounge, after speaking to Don, to walk into the kitchen with a tray of crockery.

The moment she walked through the door there was a tremendous crash of breaking glass.

The cameras kept turning. No one took any notice. As far as the viewers were concerned I imagine they assumed Carolyn had dropped the tray—and probably got a laugh out of it.

What they didn't know was that one of the overhead arc lamps had come loose and had dropped to the studio floor—missing Carolyn by inches.

It all happened out of camera vision but the noise was faithfully recorded on the sound track.

And that is how the programme went out, with the crash accepted as part of *Crossroads*.

Another top comedian, Stan Stennett, played a character role on television for the first time with us.

George Bartram, his manager, suggested the Welsh comic for a role in *Crossroads* to Reg Watson.

'I naturally expected to be given a comedy part,' said Stan. 'After all, I've been a working comic all my life. I've never done anything else.'

But Reg saw Stan in a very different light and asked him if he would be prepared to try a dramatic role.

Stan was surprised—and flattered.

'If you think I can do it—then I'll have a shot,' he said.

When the script arrived, Stan found he had been given a very dramatic role indeed; he was to play a gunman on the run who held up Mrs Hope and her husband in their cottage —at gunpoint—as hostages.

He made quite an impact and surprised his show business associates with his performance. His dramatic début with us paid off handsomely and led to another appearance on television—also as an actor.

George Bartram heard that Colin Welland had written a play with an industrial background for the BBC's *Play for Today* series. It was called *Leeds United* and was to be shot on location in Yorkshire.

Another well-known music hall comic—Bill Maynard— had already scored heavily in Welland's hit play *Kisses at Fifty* (voted Best Play for 1973 by the Society of Film and Television Arts).

So Bartram contacted the producer, told him of Stennett's success with us, and our *Crossroads* gunman finished up with a part in *Leeds United* as a shop steward.

I have told you some of the real life, unrehearsed dramas that happen in our *Crossroads* studios of which the public knows nothing, but we also have a great deal of fun.

One recording of the show was taking place at the same time as the board of ATV were having their monthly meeting at Birmingham.

This particular scene involved Janice and Bryan Jarvis arriving at their new flat and the door had to open as they walked in.

Everything went well during the day but at the dress rehearsal the door opened and all ATV's directors, including Sir Lew Grade, came through the door and marched into the studio.

We had no idea they were there. They had crept into the studio as a joke to surprise us all.

Later on, the same set provided the scene for another practical joke on Reg Watson.

The Design Department had been asked to provide this flat for Brian and Janice (David Fennell and Carolyn Lyster) and the actual details had been left to them.

The couple were just starting their TV married life together, so all that was really required was a rather small apartment.

However the scenic people came up with a very splendid set—bay windows, Gothic arches, and that sort of thing. The outside sequences for their apartment had been shot in the grounds of the Château Impney hotel at Droitwich—a very grand building which was built as a copy of a French château by a wealthy Midlands industrialist and is now a prosperous hotel.

In the interests of accuracy, our Design Department had produced a set which showed the inside of the apartment to have similar Gothic architecture.

'It looks like a grand opera,' someone giggled. And this gave us the cue to play a joke on Reg.

We all went along to Wardrobe and got ourselves fitted out in medieval costumes—just the kind of outfits you would expect to find on the stage of Covent Garden or La Scala, Milan, during a Grand Opera season.

On top of this, we arranged for an operatic tape to be played over the studio speakers—the *March of the Torea-*

dors. Then at the moment the cameras were all set for another sequence inside the Jarvis's new home during the dress rehearsal, we all marched on the set as though we were singing in Grand Opera.

It really was very funny. And quite a shock for Reg, looking down on us from his control room.

We once had a scene involving some pigeons. The idea was that someone had to open the pigeon loft, take out one of the birds, and remove a message from its leg.

At the dress rehearsal something went wrong and, instead of taking out one bird, all the pigeons flew out. The rest of the rehearsal time was spent rounding them up—all thirty of them. They were recaptured and put back in the loft—all except one.

But the recording still had to start on schedule so we went ahead, despite the fluttering of the pigeon as he flew around overhead. Luckily for us, that pigeon behaved himself. Goodness knows what you would have all thought if Meg had suddenly been covered with bird droppings while greeting a new guest.

Another occasion involved a tame fox which the manager, Nick Van Doren, was supposed to have brought into the motel. For the purpose of this particular scene the fox was required to get out of a bed and walk across the floor. I never quite understood how all this could be explained to a fox. At rehearsals it just didn't happen—the fox stayed in the bed and wouldn't move.

We decided to go ahead and the actors involved were told to make up some words to fit the situation if the fox didn't perform as required.

As it happened, everything worked perfectly—much to everyone's astonishment. At the right moment the fox *did* leave the bed and walk across the bedroom floor, just as we wanted.

I have often been asked how we managed this but the truth is I don't know. Nor does anyone else. It just happened.

But it was Tim Jones and Alan Coleman—our first two

directors—who played the classic joke of all time on our producer, Reg Watson.

We had a mystery involving sudden death going at the time—a touch of Agatha Christie. Perhaps you wouldn't expect this kind of mystery in a show such as ours but those of you who are regular viewers know how varied our plots and story lines have become over the years.

Originally we wanted a murder mystery but as *Crossroads* is for family viewing, the Independent Television Authority stepped in and told us we couldn't have a murder at a time when young children might be watching. They would, however, approve an accidental death providing no actual body appeared on the screen.

It took some ingenuity to overcome their ban and this is how we managed it.

Our plot was centred on a mysterious stranger who booked into the motel, wearing a gold ring in the shape of a skull. Viewers saw the man's arrival and then the skull was shown in close-up. When the death had taken place, instead of showing the dead man's body, it was sufficient to show the skull ring again for viewers to know at once the victim's identity.

Tim and Alan decided to liven things up a little and hired Tina—one of the chimps used in the Brooke Bond TV commercials and whom we had already used in a previous episode—at a cost of £10 for a couple of hours, plus transport.

Reg was directing this particular episode and, without him knowing anything about it but with all the cast in on the plot, they smuggled the chimp on to the *Crossroads* set and, in place of the murder victim, put Tina at the bar with a glass of orange juice and the skull ring on her finger. As an added touch, they had the chimp in full evening dress.

The camera team had been warned not to film what was going to happen for, in addition to having the chimpanzee at the bar, Tim and Alan had also made a special recording of the detective's remark when he arrived at the motel.

214

The CID man was supposed to say, 'I want to speak to Gerald Bailey please.'

But the two jokers had taped a special Larry Grayson version—in a lisping, camp manner which, in itself, was so unexpected that they knew when Reg heard it in the control room he would be flabbergasted.

It all worked perfectly. Reg was at his control panels. He cued in the actor to make his appearance. He did so—but instead of a crisp CID voice there was the lisping, 'I want to speak to Gerald Bailey please.'

Reg couldn't believe his ears. Then he looked and saw a monkey sitting at the bar.

We all waited for him to say something—but he didn't say a word.

The scene came to an end. He watched it all quietly on the TV monitors in the control room and when the final captions had faded he turned to one of his assistants and said, 'Did you see a monkey at the bar?'

The girl looked at him—convulsed with laughter.

'Yes,' she replied. 'I did.'

'Thank God, I thought I was going mad,' said Reg.

The entire studio then burst into laughter and Reg eventually joined in.

He told me afterwards that he really did think he was suffering from an hallucination when he first saw the chimpanzee and when no one else said anything about it but carried on normally he was convinced he must have been the only one seeing it.

There is one strange, off-screen story about *Crossroads* which involves my former home at Weir End, Ross-on-Wye. This was a beautiful Georgian manor house standing in its own grounds but I found I spent so little time there that I decided to take a large flat in Birmingham and this is where I now live—with Mother in her own flat, right next door.

At this time, however, Mother was living at Weir End during the week and I joined her at week-ends.

In one of our *Crossroads* episodes we had just started a situation where two tramps were planning to rob the motel for no better reason than that one of them wanted to spend the winter in jail.

We were all working away in the studios as usual one Thursday morning when Joy Andrews was called to the telephone.

The caller said, 'Joy Andrews? You don't know me but you must tell someone. They're going to rob Meg tomorrow. Please, Mrs Hope ... do something to stop them.'

It was a woman's voice and she spoke with a strong Scottish accent.

Joy was obviously puzzled, especially as the woman first used her real name and then called her Mrs Hope, and she told both Reg and me about the phone call.

We all thought the call must be from a viewer who had seen the earlier episode in which the robbery had been discussed—and was taking it for real.

The strange sequel to this is that, the following day, burglars broke into Weir End and I was the victim of a robbery in real life.

A number of articles were stolen. The CID questioned Joy Andrews about the phone call and they even appealed, over Scottish Television, to whoever had phoned the studios to come forward and promised to keep her identity a secret if she would assist them in their enquiries.

But nothing more was heard of the mysterious caller and although this happened some while ago, it remains one of the real-life mysteries of *Crossroads*.

None of us know whether the caller was really trying to warn me or whether she was getting too much involved with the make-believe robbery that was about to take place on the TV screen—just as many of our *Crossroads* fans have identified.

It was all very mystifying.

Joy Andrews has played three other characters in the serial before settling down as Mrs Hope.

Her first appearance was as a receptionist in a hairdressing salon; then she was the mother of an air hostess who was planning a secret wedding.

For her third appearance she was engaged to play the part of a rather shady hairdresser who got involved with one of the male guests at the motel. This would have been built up into quite a strong situation but when she arrived at the studios she found the actor who had been booked to play opposite her had fallen sick. So Reg fitted her into the serial in a much smaller part and told her to wear a black wig.

'Just play this little cameo for me,' he told her, 'and then we'll bring you back again in a worthwhile role as soon as we can. If you wear the wig no one will recognize you when you return.'

Reg was as good as his word, and Joy was later to create the part of Mrs Hope, mother of the new young vicar.

When her agent telephoned her about the part he told her, 'You'll have to age up a bit. You're to play the vicar's mother.'

At that time the only vicar we had was the Rev. Guy Atkins, played by the veteran actor Arnold Ridley of *Dad's Army* fame, who is in his late seventies.

'Goodness,' said Joy. 'I will have to age if I'm to be *his* mother.'

However when she arrived in Birmingham for the first reading all was explained and she was introduced to the young and handsome Rev. Peter Hope (Neville Hughes) who was to take over from the Rev. Guy Atkins on his retirement.

Chris Douglas, nineteen, is one of our latest recruits—as the seemingly no-good wastrel, Martin Bell.

He seems to be getting involved, in the plot, with Sally Adcock, who plays a waitress. Though whether anything will come of their relationship none of us has any idea— not even Chris and Sally.

217

'I'd like to think it will blossom,' he says. 'She's a sweet girl, really.'

Chris is a self-taught actor. At fifteen, he was sweeping the stage at a little theatre in Porthcawl, South Wales, for £9 a week.

'I just couldn't wait until I was old enough to go to drama school,' he says.

After Porthcawl, he got a job with the grand title of Technical Assistant Stage Manager at the Bristol Old Vic which, in reality, says Chris, was that of a glorified tea maker. Pay—£17 a week.

Spells in various small repertory companies followed at Worcester, Ilfracombe, and Swindon where he, among other things, played the back end of a horse in *Toad of Toad Hall*.

When he joined us he was supposed to be a sixteen-year-old—and said so in the programme. Then because he was later required to serve drinks behind the bar, the writers had to hope everyone had forgotten this earlier mention of being sixteen. They jumped a year and gave him a quick birthday to make him eighteen. So that's his *Crossroads* age now—eighteen.

Already Chris has learned to cope with emergencies. Earlier this year he had a scene in which he was eating some old sausages which he had taken from the motel pantry. He didn't bother to put them in his mouth during rehearsals but on the transmission he took a big bite of one of the sausages—and was nearly sick.

However, he managed to control his features, pretend all was well and that he was enjoying every mouthful, and continued the scene. Then when the camera moved away from him and he was out of vision he spat the whole lot out on the studio floor.

'I just couldn't help myself,' he explained. 'These sausages are too awful—they're rancid.'

In another scene, he was mixing shampoo in a bucket for Vera's hairdressing salon. The idea was that the shampoo should bubble over.

At rehearsals, the shampoo remained as flat as a pancake.

'Don't worry,' said one of the studio staff. 'We're putting some special stuff in the bucket to make sure it bubbles when it comes to the actual take.'

And that's what they did. I never did find out what they put into that bucket but when it came to the transmission and Chris was mixing the shampoo, the whole lot exploded ...

The studio was covered with foam and Chris looked like a fugitive from a Mack Sennett custard-pie comedy. But it all looked very funny on the screen so the director left it in ...

Jean Bayless and I were in pantomime together at the London Palladium with Terry Thomas in *Humpty Dumpty* nineteen years ago. We used to sing each other love songs for Jean was principal girl and I was principal boy, so we both had something of a giggle when she turned up at the *Crossroads* motel—in overalls—to work as Meg Richardsons cook.

'What a come down!' I joked. 'I promise not to work you too hard.'

Jean, who is the wife of a Midlands garage owner, had been introduced to Reg Watson by Janet Hargreaves (who plays Ronnie Hunter's ex-wife).

'It's silly for you to be sitting around all day with nothing to do—why not try for a job on *Crossroads*?' Janet suggested.

Over lunch in our canteen, Reg discussed what kind of role Jean might like to play and when she mentioned she was a good cook Reg said, 'Great, we'll put you in the *Crossroads* kitchen.'

So red-haired Jean became TV's Cynthia Cunningham. We have had many laughs together and I hope she will be returning to us soon.

There was one moment when, during transmission, she was supposed to say, 'I must act my age.'

This was her cue to me and this was the line for which I was waiting.

A blank look passed across Jean's face. Nothing came. No words. Nothing ...

Then just when I was about to cover up for her, Jean smiled sweetly and said, 'Meg, it's all the rage.'

I can't remember what I said in reply but, whatever it was, it must have been appropriate for the director let us carry on. There were no retakes, even though Jean's words to me had no relation to what was written in the script.

The scene ended. I threw a serviette at her ... and we both laughed.

Such awful moments, when one is completely tongue-tied, can hit the most experienced performer.

Jean did a good job for us—and carries the scars to prove it.

In one scene, she was slicing an onion in the kitchen when she cut off a quarter of an inch from the top of her thumb. As the camera was on her, she just put the piece of flesh in her overall pocket ... and carried on.

As soon as the take was finished we rushed her to first aid—with the blood gushing everywhere.

Naturally we were all very sympathetic and congratulated her on her bravery, including Reg Watson. But later, out of Jean's hearing, he took me on one side and mildly suggested that what Jean *should* have done was to register pain and horror.

'Then we could have gone on filming and included the accident on the screen. Good dramatic stuff. We might even have left them wondering as to whether she would lose her thumb, or not ...'

'Oh, Reg,' I said. 'How could you?'

But I still have a feeling he was serious.

Jean was also badly burned and blistered her fingers during her *Crossroads* role, just as she was handing a couple of plates from the stove to Amy Turtle who was waiting for them with a tray.

The plates had been heating during rehearsals and no one had remembered to switch off the hot plate so at the actual recording they were red hot.

Again Jean didn't show any sign ...

You wouldn't have found me quite so brave—or dedicated.

Mrs Cunningham has now returned to being Jean Bayless again—in a summer show last year at the Congress Theatre, Eastbourne, with Ronnie Corbett and Kenneth McKellar.

Crossroads has brought her back into the limelight, just as it has for many other experienced performers.

For although *Crossroads* will continue to give young unknown actors and actresses their first chance on television, there will always be roles for some of the many fine character players for which British drama is famed.

Whether you come to work at *Crossroads* or are just looking in ... you are all very welcome at Meg's motel.

END

A PERSONAL POSTSCRIPT

Next Spring, 1975, Meg marries Hugh Mortimer.

It will be the greatest TV wedding of all time.

The decision for Meg and Hugh to wed has been made by Jack Barton, our new producer, who has taken over from Reg Watson.

Between ourselves, I never thought it would happen but we have had so many letters and so many cards for all you *Crossroads* admirers asking for Meg and Hugh to marry that, really, we couldn't hold out any longer.

As you will know by now, John Bentley and I are very fond of each other but there is no real life romance between us. At the same time, we have always felt that a TV wedding would be in keeping with our closer relationship on the screen which is developing weekly now that Hugh has come back to *Crossroads*.

The wedding itself will be a most lavish affair. We plan to have it in Birmingham Cathedral, with actors playing the part of the clergy and the whole *Crossroads* cast present in the congregation.

We are also making arrangements to pack the pews with *Crossroads* fans.

Before the ceremony there will be a drive through the streets of Birmingham with a police escort so that as many of you as possible can see Meg in her bridal outfit.

Afterwards, Meg and Hugh will drive in an open car, with police outriders on motor cycles, back through the streets to a champagne wedding reception at ATV's Studio Centre in Birmingham.

Jack Barton tells me he will make Meg's marriage 'the biggest TV wedding ever seen. All the stops will be out.

Crossroads is a Birmingham programme and we will invite the whole city to join in.'

As Mrs Hugh Mortimer there will be many dramatic situations involving Hugh's determination to continue with his world-wide business interests.

I can visualize many wives identifying themselves with Meg's feelings when Hugh goes off, leaving her to run the motel alone.

But the essence of *Crossroads* is realism and now that Meg and Hugh have decided to share their September Love, such separations must be accepted as part of the pattern of their lives.

Nearly ten years have passed since their first meeting ...

Hugh now has a touch of grey at his temples. When Meg is his wife she will be keeping an eye on that tummy of his while Hugh, in his turn, will be taking an extra interest in how Meg looks and what she wears.

After ten years we are all a little older. Jill, my TV daughter, was a schoolgirl when we started. Now she is an elegant young matron with a family.

Sandy had a schoolcap and blazer. Today, although crippled, he leads a full life as a young man who, in a couple of years will be celebrating his thirtieth birthday.

And now Meg is to find the true happiness that every woman needs ... to marry the man she loves.

Her life as a widow is coming to an end and a new one is starting.

This is what *Crossroads* is all about—the simple straightforward story of human relationships, screened four evenings a week for 14,000,000 viewers ... a staggering total of 56,000,000 a week.

We have never pretended to present a dramatic masterpiece. We're not offering a TV epic. There is no attempt to compete with big scale, expensive productions such as you get from *Edward VII, the Forsythes*, or *Jennie*.

Instead, our stories are much closer to the lives that you and I lead in our own homes. We present events and

223

happenings related to day-to-day occurrences with which our enormous viewing audience is at once familiar.

Crossroads has never offered escapism. It deals with people like you and me and as I have tried to show in these pages, a great deal of thought, preparation, and integrity goes into its presentation.

Those of us making *Crossroads* have always been proud of this and I hope that by taking you behind the scenes we are all much closer to you at home.

For it's the welcome that you, our viewers, have given *Crossroads* these past ten years that has made possible not only the TV life of Meg Richardson but also the professional careers of everyone associated with the programme—both on and off the screen.

Without your loyalty, support, and friendship *Crossroads* could never have lasted. Even Meg could never have married ...

Thank you all and God Bless You.

NOELE GORDON